Preacher, Prophet, Poet

A Biography of Wallace E. Chappell

by

C. Emory Burton

Emory Burton (1959 GBI grad

authorHOUSE

1663 Liberty Drive, Suite 200
Bloomington, Indiana 47403
(800) 839-8640
www.AuthorHouse.com

© 2004 C. Emory Burton
All Rights Reserved.

No part of this book may be reproduced, stored in a retrieval system, or transmitted by any means without the written permission of the author.

First published by AuthorHouse 01/19/05

ISBN: 1-4184-9462-3 (sc)

Printed in the United States of America
Bloomington, Indiana

This book is printed on acid-free paper.

Table of Contents

Preface vii

Introduction ix

Chapter 1: A Story 1

Chapter 2: Family 5

Chapter 3: Childhood and Youth 8

Chapter 4: College and Marriage 14

Chapter 5: Theology 24

Chapter 6: The Board of Education 31

Chapter 7: Surviving a Crisis 40

Chapter 8: Thoughts on the Church 46

Chapter 9: Cochran Chapel 51

Chapter 10: And the Walls Come Tumbling Down: a sermon 56

Chapter 11: Later Ministry 63

Chapter 12: Colorado and Back 70

Chapter 13: Reflections 75

Chapter 14: The God of the Mountains (a sermon) 83

Appendix: Poetry 90

Afterword 114

Related Reading 116

Glossary of Terms 118

Preface

A remarkable United Methodist minister, Wallace E. ("Wally") Chappell of Dallas, Texas, never served an extremely large church and was never elected a bishop, but his life has left a significant mark on Methodism, particularly in the state of Texas. His career is a model for anyone interested in the role of the minister and the contemporary Church, particularly in the Methodist tradition.

The story of Wally Chappell represents the "progressive tradition" in his denomination and in society as a whole. While some people associate religion--especially in the Southern Protestant tradition--with ultraconservative theological and political views, Chappell has always championed progressive ideas, and has spoken his views courageously in a conservative environment. Chapter 5 outlines his views on theology and Chapter 13 includes his reflections on a range of contemporary issues.

In an age in which the role of the Church has come into question in the eyes of some, Chappell presents a strong defense of the Church and a ringing challenge to it as well. Is the purpose of the Church primarily individual salvation, or should it speak out on community, national, and international issues? Is the Church primarily a local organization or club, or does it have an inherent tie to the larger body of the church? Chappell's thoughts on the church are in Chapter 8.

In addition to specifically theological and ecclesiastical matters, Chappell has notable ideas on personal and spiritual growth, and on making the most of one's life, which are significant to those of both religious and nonreligious persuasions. His concerns for personal health and physical fitness are as relevant as his ideas for personal and spiritual growth.

An insight Chappell exemplifies is the lifting of our vision from narrow, parochial matters to a broad-minded, cosmopolitan outlook. A narrow perspective tends to view our group, race, social class, community, and local church as the final locus of truth. The broader viewpoint, which Chappell favors, sees people of all races and classes as significant. It views other denominations and other religions as important, and stresses a national and international perspective.

Two of Chappell's sermons are in Chapter 10 and Chapter 14, and a bicycle ride from Dallas to Colorado is described in Chapter 12. Some of his poems are introduced at relevant places, and an appendix has a collection of others. Related reading and a glossary of United Methodist terminology are included.

I would like to thank all those who assisted in the writing of this book. John Fiedler and the staff of the First United Methodist Church of Dallas were encouraging. Betty Balliet assisted in evaluating the poems. Alice Peppler of Chicago, Illinois, read most of the manuscript and made many helpful suggestions. Thanks to Bishop William Oden for taking the time to write an introduction, and to Darryl Wilbanks for most of the photographs. My wife, Dorothy, suggested the subject for the book and was patient during its completion. Most of all, I would like to express appreciation to Wally and Stell Chappell for their interviews and cooperation in this project.

Introduction

Wally Chappell is a unique resource of Christianity, especially the United Methodist Church, and even more specifically, the North Texas Annual Conference.

Emory Burton has done all of us a favor by highlighting the person and work of Wally.

Wally Chappell is a true renaissance man—theologian, scholar, poet, lover of nature, social activist. He is an individualist who also knows the value of institutional power—when used for the good. Wally and his wife Stell are both committed to social causes affirmed by our *Social Principles*.

Pastors and seminarians could find an excellent model of how to affirm the connection at every level and at the same time faithfully call into question issues of justice.

I especially appreciated Burton's including samples of Wally's preaching. Wally's life, theology, activism, and fervor all come together in his sermons. There is homiletical gold to mine in Chappell's sermons.

When I receive a letter or report that begins with "Dear Chief," I know I am in for both a treat and a challenge. Readers of Burton's book will find the same.

William B. Oden, Bishop
Dallas area
The United Methodist Church

x

Chapter 1: A Story

Al Slaton, born in a rural slum in Oklahoma in 1932, managed to get into about as much trouble as one could in his early years. He used drugs regularly, conned people out of money, and was in and out of prison several times. He himself described his life, associating as he did with riffraff and hoodlums, as a jungle. "I had never met anyone in the straight world," he admits.

In 1958, WFAA-TV in Dallas presented a program on crime and rehabilitation, after which criminals were paired with leading citizens from the community. Al Slaton, fresh out of prison and a person with no friends, was paired with Dallas minister Wally Chappell.

After the program, Chappell asked Slaton to come have dinner with him and his wife, which he did. Chappell was able to accept Slaton as a person, and looking beyond the criminal exterior, saw a likeable person with some potential. Neither would have thought it at the time, but this was the beginning of a 40-plus year friendship.

Despite Chappell's mentoring and counsel, Slaton did not change right away. He still had, in his own terms, a "psychopathic mind." He continued to use drugs and steal, and eventually found himself in prison again. But Chappell never gave up on Slaton, visiting him in prison, offering counsel, helping him find employment, and writing letters on his behalf.

After Slaton was released from prison, he joined the Ridgewood Park United Methodist Church where Chappell was the minister, and came to know Jess Hay, prominent attorney and member of the church. But Al had not forsaken his old ways. Not only did he stay in trouble with the law, but he would let himself into the church on weekdays and bring girls and drugs. Although he seemed to be responding to Chappell's guidance, he was having difficulty making the moral connections.

Over time, however, his life began to turn around. He was employed as a nurses' aid in a Veterans Administration hospital in Waco, Texas. Unfortunately, he began to associate with some rough characters. One evening, when Slaton and three others were out cruising around, one of the other men expressed the desire to kill a cop. A confrontation developed between this man and Slaton, and Al shot and killed the man. He hid the body, but his conscience bothered him and the next day he went to the police with the story.

Defense lawyer Warren Burnett was persuaded to take Slaton's case. Burnett, using a plea of self-defense, enabled Slaton to avoid prison. This disturbing incident, along with Chappell's continued guidance, may have been the catalyst that turned his life around, for he was able to break his drug habit and lift the vision for his life.

Slaton had developed a fierce, intense feeling for the underdog. In the VA hospital, he reported that some attendants were abusing patients. The report was investigated and the superintendent was fired.

After he began to work in a hospital in Temple, Texas, Slaton got the idea of establishing a home for mentally ill people. About this time, state hospitals had cut loose many patients, increasing the ranks of the homeless. Slaton bought an old house in Temple as a home for ex-convicts and the mentally ill. Over the next 25 years, he bought several houses for this purpose, never turning away anyone who needed a place to stay..

As of 2004 Slaton has 10 houses, known as The Rose Garden, which house 65 people. He has had considerably difficulty abiding by all the state regulations. Once the state raided the homes, rounded up the residents, shot their pets in front of them, and caused considerable disarray. Chappell has intervened on Slaton's behalf on several occasions, and Jess Hay, the Dallas attorney, has

Preacher, Prophet, Poet

contributed generously to the program. Chappell has been most impressed with Slaton's compassion, and deems him the most unforgettable character of his life.

In a letter written to a judge in defense of The Rose Garden, Chappell pointed out that in almost 20 years, no one staying in the facilities has ever had to go back to prison. While the facility has not always met state regulations, the truth is that *no licensed facility will accept most of these people.* "The Rose Garden is rendering society a most valued service in providing care for people that *no one else* in the care business wants."

"I have known Al Slaton for 40 years, in and out of prison, on and off drugs, wild and straight, and finally as a highly productive citizen who deserves our praise. I know him well. He is an amazing person with an amazing gift for ministering to marginalized people. I believe him to be a completely honest person. ...I write this in the strong hope that in your court you will find justice, a major element in the biblical faith that I espouse."

As I arrived at Al Slaton's home in Temple, he introduced me to his son, a black man of 17 or 18. The story behind this is that when Slaton heard that a woman in Huntsville (Texas) prison was going to have a baby, he went there and convinced the authorities that he was the woman's uncle, took the baby, legally adopted him, and has been raising him as his son ever since.

Slaton talked openly with me for over an hour. "I would not be sitting here today except for Wally Chappell. He opened doors and motivated me. He has been a companion in good times and bad, when I was in prison, on the streets, a drug addict. He never betrayed me."

Slaton realized that he didn't talk the language Chappell did. "Wally had never been around people like me." Chappell invited Slaton into his home, allowed him to babysit his boys. "I got to know him and his family, and a lot of trust was being built. He took me in almost like Jesus Christ." Slaton later named one of his sons Wally Chappell Slaton.

Chappell put Slaton in touch with the "dirty dozen," the group of committed Methodist ministers in Dallas. "They were following the teachings of Jesus," says Slaton, "reaching out to the poor and hungry.

"Here was a man I could trust: honest, sincere, clear minded. He taught me about true love and true feelings." Even when Slaton stayed on drugs, Chappell, while disapproving of his bad habits, continued his support and fellowship.

"Wally was my spiritual adviser and friend. It's a great thing to go through life and meet a true friend. When my mother died in 1958, he took me to her funeral in Oklahoma. When I was diagnosed with terminal cancer (in 2002), he was there at my bedside. He has written me hundreds of letters. He has visited me many times in prison; he was always trying to help me. He was always motivating me to do the right thing, to pursue my dreams."

After describing some of the programs at Rose Garden, Slaton noted that Chappell was instrumental in many of them. "I've never met anyone like Wally Chappell. He reaches out to people at the bottom and relates to them. There is no hypocrisy there. He sees good in everyone, and has a love for all people. He is the most unforgettable character I've ever known. I strongly believe in God and prayer and Wally Chappell."

Chapter 2: Family

It's only about a three-mile drive from my house to Wally's. As I drove up to the pleasant but modest home in the quiet, tree-lined neighborhood, I noticed a large oak tree in the front yard. Wally had planted that tree many years ago. The word "Peace" was on the front door, a word that seemed to symbolize Wally's manner and lifestyle.

I was here for the first of what would be some ten interviews with the Reverend Wallace Chappell, the man everyone calls "Wally." He offered me a cup of coffee—a gesture that would become routine over the next several weeks—and made me feel entirely comfortable as we talked. A tall man, large but not obese, with white hair and brown eyes, his manner and bearing belied his 83 years.

Here was a man who undoubtedly was very busy. He was employed by the First United Methodist Church of Dallas, he had several projects going, including ministerial trips to the women's prison in Fort Worth, yet showed no dismay that I was taking an hour or more of his time. He answered my questions without false modesty, but with no suggestion of arrogance. He stopped occasionally and asked me about my experiences in the ministry, which paralleled his to a degree.

When I asked Wally about his family background, I learned that he had a remarkable set of parents, Frank and Pearl Wallace. Here are their stories and those of their respective parents.

Frank Wilson Chappell, born in 1881, was the second son of E. B. Chappell, a distinguished leader in the Methodist Church. E. B. Chappell was a Sunday school editor for 20 years, and served several churches in Texas and Tennessee. After three years at LaGrange, a Texas mission, and a church in San Antonio, he served a fellowship in Austin that became the First Methodist Church. Later a ministry included a downtown church in St. Louis, a four-year pastorate at McKendree Church in Nashville, Tennessee, and service on the Methodist General Board of Education.

Although no grandparent had a strong influence on him, Wally remembers spending some time with E. B. Chappell, and a few visits with his paternal grandmother, Jennie Headlee Chappell.

Frank attended high school in Nashville and studied engineering at Vanderbilt University. (Around 1900 only about two percent of the population went to college.) Frank Chappell received the bachelor of engineering degree in 1903. Meticulous and organized, he was considered a very good man with splendid integrity. He kept good files and records, and soaked up respect in his profession. He stayed in engineering until he retired at the age of 84; he died in 1968 at the age of 87.

Among the projects Frank Chappell designed in the Dallas area were the Cotton Bowl, the Lifestock Coliseum, the Automotive Building, and the renovation of the music hall. He designed most of the postwar buildings at Southern Methodist University (SMU) and pacesetting apartments at 3525 Turtle Creek, the first structure of its type in the Southwest. He was active in Highland Park Methodist Church, Dallas, for 50 years, a loved and respected man.

Pearl Wallace was born in 1888, the daughter of Jesse and Belle Wallace. Jesse was a circuit rider from Arkansas, a joyous, happy man with a good sense of humor, which became part of the family tradition. (This trait certainly carried down to Wally!) Jesse's wife, Belle Harrell, was deaf, devout, and rigid. At that time, a Methodist minister had to "locate" (retire) when he had too many children, so Jesse and Belle settled in Dallas around 1903 where he worked as a carpenter. Wally has some recollections of his maternal grandparents, although Belle died when he was only 16.

Pearl was born into a family of four daughters (she was the second) and two sons. She completed high school after her father relocated to Dallas. All the women of this family were intelligent and gifted. A poet at heart, Pearl became a speech teacher with an emphasis on expression and elocution. She also was a drama coach and writer for many years, and was reputed to be one of the top book reviewers in Dallas. She died in early 1969, less than two years after the death of her husband. It is hardly surprising that Wally says the greatest influence on his life was that of his mother.

An amusing story about Pearl Chappell has survived. One Sunday afternoon she attended a music program at Fair Park Auditorium in Dallas. At intermission she was outside in the hall and encountered someone that she knew. Without really thinking she said, "I know your name, now what is your face?"

Frank and Pearl, married in 1915, had three children. Their oldest, Frank Chappell, Jr., was a medical journalist for the news bureau of the American Medical Association for 25 years. The youngest was a daughter, Ethel Chappell Glenn, who lives in Greensboro, North Carolina. She earned an M. A. and doctorate from the University of Texas and taught speech and communications at the University of North Carolina at Greensboro for 23 years.

Both parents provided loving but not harsh discipline. It was their high expectations for their children that motivated both sons and the daughter to do their best in whatever they attempted.

This book is about Frank and Pearl Wallace's second child, Wallace Edwin Chappell. Named for an uncle, he was born on St. Patrick's Day, March 17, 1920. Probably no one could have guessed that this child would grow up to make the most of his talents, to lead a remarkably varied and interesting life, and would influence hundreds—indeed thousands—of people until well into the twenty-first century.

Chapter 3: Childhood and Youth

I suppose most of us have fond memories of our childhood, and this is certainly true for Wally. His happy childhood may have been due to a combination of great parents, an older brother to emulate, a challenging physical environment, and stimulating religious training. Not even the Great Depression—commencing when Wally was about nine—did much to dampen the exuberance of his childhood years.

The family moved to the University Park section of Dallas when Wally was five. They lived near SMU, and across the alley were farmlands, woods, and an old barn, which lent something of a rural atmosphere to city living. Frank and Wally fantasized that they were great woodsmen. Both spent great times tramping the woods and creeks and making tree houses. Wally once saw an English bulldog fighting with a cotton-mouth moccasin (the bulldog finally won!). Experiences like these helped develop a sensitivity to the created world.

Frank and Wally discovered that an old barn across the alley was infested with pigeons. They took advantage of the situation by sneaking over at night, sacking several pigeons, and having a pigeon roast.

They built tree houses and cleaned out brush on the ground to create the appearance of a cave. At least once Wally got poison ivy from the waist up, covering his arms. He drank water from the creek and later wondered why he didn't get sick.

There was a pond at Lovers Lane (a street nearby) where Wally learned to swim. One day he followed Frank across the pond until the water got over his head, and then dog-paddled the rest of the way by instinct.

Big brother Frank always seemed to take good care of him. When Wally was very young, Frank would read and he would listen. Both mowed yards to make money, then take the streetcar and go to the fairgrounds. Wally learned to keep a nickel in his shoe so he would be sure to have money to catch the streetcar home.

Wally has fewer memories of his little sister, some six years his junior. He does recall that by the age of eight or ten, Ethel showed much talent in creating puppet shows. By the time she grew up, according to Wally, she was the smartest of the three children.

The only school in town at that time was Armstrong School. Wally attended it until Bradfield School was completed and then transferred. The teacher, Mrs. Phillips, had divided the class into an A and a B section. Presumably the A section was the superior one, and Wally understood that was the group he was in. One day she instructed the A group to get out its materials, and Wally began to comply. She said, "Not you, Wallace, I put you in the B group." He recalls being absolutely crushed, an incident that undoubtedly affected his self-esteem.

The church was a strong, positive experience for Wally from the beginning. As a boy, he was influenced by several Sunday school teachers, including Mrs. Francis in the primary department and Mrs. Leisy in junior high. Even Wally's early experiences were positive and challenging, never the negative, puritanical, guilt-inducing theology that may warp the minds of young people.

His father, an engineer, would build such things as steps and ramps, and had an interest in tinkering with things. His interest carried over to his son, for Wally could fix most things except something electrical. He also loved mechanical drawing and was fascinated by things like floor plans.

One of his fond memories of his father was the time they built a "konine kite" together. The kite was about four feet tall and flew 30 or 40 feet off the ground, not a dazzling feat but a delight for a youngster.

His mother was a highly literary person, interested in drama. She also felt deeply about issues and causes, and her voice and manner reflected this. She would sometimes cast Wally in plays in church or community events. He recalls playing the dog "Nana" in *Peter Pan*, grey hair all over his face.

The Great Depression hit hard in the 1930s. Youth today can hardly appreciate the difficulties of living in that era. And conditions were worse in the South than in most other regions. Unemployment reached 25 percent and those fortunate enough to have jobs usually made less than $100 a month. I remember hearing a man explain the great lengths one would take to avoid buying something new: for example, if one needed some bolts, he might go into his garage and take bolts off old equipment, rather than pay 20 or 30 cents for new ones.

Wally's father lost a home on two separate occasions, which left him afraid of investments. When Frank Sr. learned that his sister-in-law and mother-in-law were about to lose their house, he moved in with them, paying some rent, to help save money. (They eventually lost the house anyway.) When the gas was turned off, they cut up apple crates and other boxes to use for fuel for cooking in the back yard. There was not much in the way of clothing: Wally had one pair of shoes, one pair of pants, and very few shirts. Most of his socks didn't match; he once wore mismatched socks and explained to his friends that this was a new fad. Although they were poor, he and his family did not find the condition crushing; they maintained a certain resilience in the face of poverty.

Franklin Roosevelt took steps to ease the effects of the Depression. One of his best-known programs was the Works Progress Administration. A division of the WPA, the Public Works Administration, expanded federally sponsored public works projects to provide employment and stimulate the economy. Wally's father found employment as an engineer with the PWA, working for the city of Austin and the University of Texas.

In 1934 Frank Jr. left to enroll in the University of Texas, and Wally moved into a huge rooming house with his mother and sister. His mother used the basement of the house for private tutoring, from which she earned small fees. To pay the rent, she taught the

Preacher, Prophet, Poet

grown daughters of the woman who owned the house. By 1935 the Chappells were beginning to emerge from the Depression.

Dallas had three newspapers at that time, *The Dallas Morning News*, *The Dallas Times-Herald*, and *The Dallas Dispatch*. Wally delivered papers for *The Dispatch*. He had to do his own collecting and meet the district manager to pay his bill. One day he folded five one-dollar bills into a tight wad, put them in his pocket, and went to pay for his papers. When he reached into his pocket to retrieve the money, it was gone, apparently having fallen out on the way. His boss did not believe his story and fired him on the spot. He cried all the way home.

But an exciting adventure of youth lay just ahead.

In the 1930s, the Park Cities and Highland Park areas were considered the elite sections of Dallas. Yet children whose fathers had blue-collar jobs attended school and played with children of professional fathers with no embarrassment. The prestigious Dallas Country Club had a fairly open policy: if someone could arrange for a member to place his name on the door, he could get in by paying a dollar. On this basis, Wally attended every Saturday night for some three and a half years.

He started dancing when he was 12 or 13 years old, and soon became a smooth ballroom dancer. (Many years later he became a folk dance teacher, recorded dances, and co-authored some well-received instructions on dance.)

Once, at age 15, he had to attend a formal dance, so he bought a tuxedo from Stein's department store for $15. He wore it out in three years. These were exciting times: he lived in a world of church, rich kids, the football team, the student council, and other activities.

Sports always had an appeal to Wally. He was tall but not big: at 15, he stood six feet tall and weighed about 130 pounds. Too small for the football team, he showed up at the football field anyway, running laps and doing calisthenics. Eventually he gained a little weight (to about 155 pounds) and by his senior year became the first-team center for the junior varsity. He was also elected president of the student council and once went to the state convention for student leaders.

C. Emory Burton

The church continued its strong influence during this period. The young minister of the Highland Park Methodist Church, Marshall Steel, was a gifted teacher-preacher and social activist (a protégé of the famed Harry Emerson Fosdick). Some considered him the outstanding minister in the Southwest. A pacifist, he influenced Wally to become a pacifist himself, though he had not thought through its implications. Margaret Wasson, daughter of a missionary, was a memorable teacher in the youth department. L. F. Sensabaugh came from the Methodist Board of Education in Nashville and led a strong youth ministry.

(In the Methodist Church, a general board is a structure that coordinates work in a specific area, such as education or missions, for the entire denomination.)

The youth organization at that time was the Epworth League, which later became the Methodist Youth Fellowship (MWF). Wally recalls that one day he went to the MYF meeting when he really didn't want to go, and that very day they elected him president. It was about then he began to think of himself as a leader.

Unlike many who were raised in a fundamentalist environment and had to struggle with this theology later, Wally grew up exposed to progressive thought. He never felt compelled to adhere to literalist views of the virgin birth and certain biblical miracles just because some orthodoxy required it. At the same time, his liberal theology had something of a pietistic cast to it: he saw a place for a warm, personal religious faith.

Mount Sequoyah Institute at the Western Methodist assembly near Fayetteville, Arkansas, presented superb conferences run by a national staff. Leaders included E. O. Harbin, author of *The Fun Encyclopedia*, and Walter Towner. Dean W. J. Faulkner from Fisk University in Nashville was a powerful black preacher who provided a great challenge to all the youth. Mount Sequoyah proved to be one of the major influences in Wally's life.

Typically, Wally's original motives in going to these conferences were simply to have some place to go and goof off. But by the third conference, he began to respond seriously to their appeal. He took the course on recreation three times and was hooked on it. This eventually led to Wally's becoming one of the authorities in the Methodist Church on the role of recreation and leisure activities.

If some consider recreation to be a casual and even superfluous aspect of church life, it must be remembered that all groups, especially those with young people in them, have some place for physical and recreational activities, and they serve as reminders of the social and group context in which the church and community exist. Later church recreation became expanded into leisure ministry, which became a significant aspect of church life in the middle and late twentieth century.

Wally had such a marvelous time in high school that when he graduated in 1938 he had mixed emotions about going to college. Would it be a letdown? Going to SMU had no appeal for him even though it had offered him a scholarship. In the fall he went to work for Southwestern Bell Telephone Company. His friend, Lawrence Prehn, was the son of the general manager of the company and had been an office boy there. When Larry announced he was going to Rice University in Houston, Wally went to the 18th floor and asked Mr. Prehn if he could be an office boy. Apparently sensing this young man's potential, the boss gave him the job on the condition that it would be for one year only; after that he had to go to college.

Chapter 4: College and Marriage

After high school graduation, Wally contemplated his future. He did not want to be a civil engineer because of the cyclic and unpredictable nature of the profession; in a downturn an engineer might be out of work. He took some night classes at SMU, but really wanted to go to college somewhere other than Dallas. When Larry told him of the chemical engineering program at Rice and added that there was no tuition, Wally made his decision. He applied at Rice University in Houston and, on the basis of three A's at SMU, was accepted.

At Rice he was president of the freshman class, on the honor roll, and active in many things. Although a fine student, theoretical material was almost his undoing. He was very good in chemistry but barely made a D in physical chemistry, and struggled to make a D in calculus. Finally he got some tutoring and learned the principle of calculus. At summer school at the University of Colorado at Boulder he made an A in that subject. With increased confidence, he finished Rice in four years.

On graduation, Wally went to work at Union Carbide, Texas City. Since he was living in Galveston, he had to commute. He worked under the War Manpower Commission, which kept technically trained personnel in industry. He was ready to join the navy, and they had asked for a release from the draft board so he could join. He wrote to ask for this, but they replied that they couldn't release anybody. For a time he felt odd that he was quite big but not in the service.

St. Paul Methodist, a beautiful church with Gothic architecture, was located about a mile from Rice. The minister at this church, Dawson Bryan, was influential on Wally in helping him make life decisions. Commuting from Galveston, Wally stayed with a friend in Houston who had a garage apartment. As soon as he graduated, he was named as counselor for the Methodist Youth Fellowship at the St. Paul church.

Always an extrovert, Wally had his share of girlfriends in both high school and college, including a romance that ended in his senior year. Then, at a youth conference at Mount Sequoyah in Arkansas, he spotted a pretty girl a few years his junior. Mary Frances Stell, from Port Arthur, Texas, had just broken up with her high school boyfriend. She had played on the high school basketball team where there was another Mary Frances, and to avoid confusion she began to go by her last name. Only her parents and one or two relatives ever called her by her first names, and Wally never called her anything but Stell. She had attended Port Arthur Business College and finished at Lon Morris, a two-year school, working part-time in shorthand and typing.

Stell was involved in many things, including Rainbow Girls, a fraternal organization sponsored by the Masonic order, one of the few organizations available for high school girls at that time. Her home church once had Robert Goodrich, senior, as its pastor. His son later served First Methodist Church of Dallas for many years before becoming a bishop. Stell was elected president of the MYF in the Texas Conference in 1944. At the Mount Sequoyah Youth Conference, Bishop Mack Stowe suggested this might be a great time for her to find a lifelong companion.

Wally fell madly in love with Stell in two days. She went to a national conference for Methodist youth in Green Lake, Wisconsin, and then came by Dallas to meet Wally's parents. Both Wally and Stell report that she fell in love with his parents before she did Wally himself.

Wally was to meet Stell at the train station in Houston, but at the agreed-upon time Wally was nowhere to be seen. Had he changed his mind? Any doubt was removed when the train pulled in late and Wally appeared.

Shortly before his relationship with Stell began to mature, a crucial event occurred in Wally's life. Late one evening, he was reading Lloyd C. Douglas' *The Robe*. Wally felt he was actually present as Douglas described the stoning of Stephen (the first Christian martyr) in such a vivid way. Then an inner voice asked him, "Who is going to do Stephen's work?" and he said aloud, "I'll do it," and closed the book, turned out the light, and went to sleep.

Wally told this to Stell (no one else), and added that he had decided to go to seminary. Stell responded that she really didn't want to marry a preacher. It took a little time to work some things out, but love prevailed.

Shortly afterwards Wally was licensed to preach at St. Paul's Church, Houston. (Being licensed to preach is a preliminary step to becoming a minister; full ordination normally occurs after seminary is completed.) At the time he was quite naïve about the structure of the Methodist Church: Someone had to tell him that you had to join an Annual Conference. (An Annual Conference is the structure involving all Methodists in a given area. A small state might have only one such conference, but a large state might have three or more. A minister who seeks an appointment—being assigned to a church or other position—must be a member of an Annual Conference.)

Since Wally and Stell had resolved their conflict about her marrying a minister, the two were married August 31, 1945, at her home church in Port Arthur. In this conservative era it was widely understood that the male was the authority figure in the family. (Stell comments wryly that she learned better later.)

Stell admired Wally's buoyant spirit, his creative talents, his love of people, and his enthusiasm for life and for the church. She does add that he could be a bit stubborn. Over the years Stell proved to be the perfect companion: in addition to enjoying church work, she spent time in crafts, making all their Christmas gifts for many years. She worked with bazaars, participated in some of the studies available at the church, and was often used as a wedding consultant.

At the end of September, 1945, Stell and Wally packed up to go to seminary at Perkins School of Theology at SMU in Dallas,

Preacher, Prophet, Poet

where they roomed with his parents. Stell had planned to go to the University of Texas, but Wally talked her into going to SMU. Wally became student assistant (something like an intern) at his old church, Highland Park Methodist, and Stell became secretary of the education office at SMU.

A year later, the church treasurer, Ed Mouzon, head of the math department at SMU, told Wally the school needed math teachers. So Wally, who had struggled with calculus not long before, taught four sections of algebra in the fall of 1946.

The experience of seminary, at least in mainline denominations such as the Methodist church, introduces students to an intellectual and sophisticated presentation of religion and its relationship to society. Learning a critical and historical approach to the Bible, seeing the place of theology in a broad philosophical framework, and appreciating insights from other religions, could be a shock to some students. Because of Wally's broad religious background in his church and at Mount Sequoyah, he adjusted well to the experience and became a fine student.

Some of the influential teachers at Perkins included James Seehorn Seneker, the Christian Education professor, who had some great ideas, Dr. Hicks in Old Testament, Wesley Davis in New Testament, and Paul Root in the sociology of religion.

Perhaps Wally's most influential teacher was Fred Gealy, a gentle and brilliant man, who taught missions and church music. He had served as a missionary in Japan for 17 years, and became one of the most popular men on the campus. (Since Wally had become quite good at handball, Gealy and he enjoyed many games together.)

Perkins was still under the influence of pietism, which stresses individual, even emotional faith. When Merrimon Cuninggim came as dean of the school in the early 1950s, the old guard began to retire. Then such names as Albert Outler, Shubert Ogden, Van Harvey, Ed Hobbs, and Joe Mathews took the stage. Mathews, whose name is associated with the Ecumenical Institute, was to have a later influence on Wally.

In May of 1947 Wally received a call from A. W. Martin, the professor who handled inter-conference relations. He said that Dr. Buddin, the district superintendent, told him they needed a student pastor at the Irwindale Church in Oak Cliff (in the western part of Dallas). This was, according to Martin, "the opportunity of a lifetime." He added that if Bishop Selecman read Wally's name at the Annual Conference, that would confirm the appointment.

Wally drove out Westmoreland Street to find the church. Perhaps because of a small sign and because half of the church was above ground and half below, Wally drove right by it without recognizing it. Finally he found the church and realized this would be his first pastorate.

An outsider to church life sometimes says that a minister works only about an hour a week. As Wally sensed but discovered firsthand, a minister has responsibility for the congregation in terms of church organization (which can be extensive in some churches), visitation, especially with those sick and in hospitals, performing weddings and funerals, keeping active in denominational programs, and participating in the life of the community.

One responsibility of a minister that can be overlooked is counseling people in need. Once word gets out that a minister is a good listener, not overly judgmental, and can keep confidences, people will contact him. Relatively few come with theological difficulties or trouble with praying. The problems they do bring to the minister run the gamut of human needs: depression, family problems, infidelity, troubles with one's job, addictions, and the like.

His experience in the human potential movement in the 50s and 60s and his understanding of human relationships made Chappell an effective counselor, though he never considered himself a trained therapist. He learned to recognize serious problems and to make referrals to more appropriate sources of help.

All Chappell knew to do at this church was to love the people, whom he found to be patient and kind. One member there, Mrs. Minor, widow of a teacher at Perkins, was a dear, intelligent, compassionate person. Once after he had preached a sermon on suffering, she commented, "Wallace, you haven't got this down yet, have you?"

And he admitted, "No, Mrs. Minor, I haven't."

At this pastorate someone donated a pool table to the church, and a few laymen objected. Stell recalls hearing Wally argue with

Preacher, Prophet, Poet

one of the laymen about this, and was shocked to hear Wally raise his voice! (The church kept the pool table.)

Stell recalls that about this time they bought a television set and the whole neighborhood came over to watch it. She remembers this church as a nurturing experience where two of their boys were born: Douglas Wilson in 1948, Lee Paul in 1950. Doug, according to Stell, was fascinated with words and relationships, much like his father and paternal grandmother.

Two of Wally's sermons were taken by *Circuit Rider* and used by Martin Marty, the well-known minister and church historian at the University of Chicago. One of them, written at the time many ministers were dropping out, was entitled "I Stick."

Now that Chappell had completed college and seminary, and had served the first of what was to be several pastorates, he could reflect on the progressive theology he had come to hold. The next chapter examines what that theology was.

Wally Chappell in 1951

Backpacking in Colorado in 1983

Bike Ride to Colorado, 1991

Chappell in the pulpit, 2004

Wally and Stell Chappell, 2004

Chappell greets layman Charles Mangum, 2004

Chappell with Emory Burton, 2004

Chapter 5: Theology

The progressive Christianity that Chappell learned as a young man emphasized a personal commitment to a meaningful life found in Jesus Christ and the church. It recognized the significance of the truths found in the Bible and in historic creeds, without being slavishly bound to them. It went beyond a personal religion to a religion that sought a better society and a better world, with special attention to the poor and forsaken in our midst.

The foundation of his theology is a God described in creeds and canon as seen by good modern scholarship: There is "Another," a Beyond in our midst, a Presence, a Power, The Source of Everything, a Spirit that Christians label God. Jesus is the revealer of God, known by many terms, including Messiah, Master, Son of God, Son of Man, "the human one." The New Testament is not clear on the mode of the Resurrection and witnesses were conflicted on it. The heart of the Resurrection is that there is an ongoing Presence that meets us in daily life.

In one of his communion sermons, Chappell said:

"When we walk with God as a father, and walk with Christ as Son and Savior, and walk with that strange Spirit companion of the way, it is to walk with an impenetrable mystery! Who comprehends God? No one. Who has it all nailed down (even the Trinity)? No one. (But) it isn't doctrine that saves, but the God who loves us, meets us, not in creeds, but in the Christ. Not even the finest, clearest orthodoxy (generally accepted beliefs) from the greatest

Preacher, Prophet, Poet

saints saves, but Christ, whom we meet in bread and wine, in love and transformation."

Yet much of what was taught in the churches contradicted this kind of progressive Christianity. A great deal of what the church had to say was framed in dogmatic absolutes, what might be called "the tyranny of orthodoxy." We were told we had to believe a certain way because someone said so. Things had to be as they used to be; our encounter with God became frozen in time. This outlook took the faith "once given to the saints" and assumed that that faith never changed. Creeds and canon were seen as the same yesterday, today, and forever, as if we must go back to them. Chappell believes it is not possible to go back to much of anything.

One of Chappell's favorite texts is the parable of the judgment (Matthew 25: 31-45), ending with the beautiful words, "Inasmuch as you have done it to one of the least of these my brethren, you have done it unto me." He notes that the text does not ask what we have believed, but what we have done.

After making a careful study of what is called heresy (a deviation from orthodoxy), Chappell was reassured to affirm that Methodism is a denomination that does not insist on its members agreeing to a long list of theological propositions beyond a few basics. We are *not* required to believe everything in the creeds. To be a Methodist is more like having a driver's license for lifetime continuing education than it is receiving a diploma for graduation to a higher humanity. To Chappell most of the ancient controversies are as dry as dust today.

In his study of ancient heresies, Chappell found that at any one time there were more heretics than there were orthodox believers. There were never more than a handful of great leaders who saw a central truth, clung to it, sometimes in the face of death, and brought Christians through to the middle course we identify today: One God, Creator, a God of grace and love, who was revealed in Jesus, whose teaching we are called to follow, who is our Savior and Lord, and who is mediated to us by the Holy Spirit.

The concept of the Trinity (God the Father, Son, and Holy Spirit) emerged slowly as early Christians tried to make sense of "the one and the many." It is a sticky, confusing notion, which some interpret almost as three distinct entities, a denial of monotheism. It's almost as if some Christians would coerce other Christians to accept their views on this doctrine. Yet Chappell affirms the general concept of the Trinity (God in three persons), noting that the Latin "persona" referred to a mask worn by an actor, meaning that God is *one* but plays different roles.

We inherited a conservative movement from frontier days, which stressed the necessity of converting people. While it may have had a place in its time, this movement was poorly suited to be adapted to a modern, urbanized society. Further, it was not well-grounded historically, not well-founded in its interpretation of Scripture, nor had it come to grips with the insights of modern science.

The concept of salvation is a necessary one, but often it is not made clear *from* what we are being saved or *to* what. It is difficult to disassociate salvation talk from otherworldly heaven-hell ideas, which have lost their reality for many. There seems to be a basic contradiction between the burning hunger for salvation (either on the part of the evangelist or the convert) and Jesus' emphasis on loving God with one's heart and mind, and loving others as oneself. "Amazing grace addresses one forgivingly, releasing me to live triumphantly for others. I concentrate on life, today, to be obedient to God's will."

Many emphasize crusades only for the sake of getting conversions, but the Christian church is more than getting converts certified! We have to sit together long enough to be Christians. The gathered aspect of community in Christ, for Chappell, is more essential than is the work for first decisions. "Do we feel we must evangelize so hard because our fellowship is not sufficiently attractive?"

Chappell once knew a man who was "saved" and began to study the Bible, teach Sunday school, and was considered something of a saint. Then it became known that he abused his wife, checked her mail, and ruled with an iron hand. There is something badly wrong with such a faith. Knowing Christ cannot be reconciled with doing violence to those in our homes.

Most of the people who ignore the faith, according to Chappell, look upon much of our Christian witness as nonsense, or self-deception, or unscientific, or irrelevant. They seem to have no experience on which to base any God claims. They look on the long and sorry history of religionists killing each other and dismiss the whole thing out of hand. For them, authoritarian answers will not work. We *have to* find new ways of enunciating meaning other than Biblical "physics," heaven and hell, reward and punishment, truth and falsehood.

Another weakness in the conservative tradition was its individualism, as reflected in revivalism. The Christian tradition consistently speaks of humans as members of communities. It is difficult to find in that tradition support for isolated individuals who are not responsible to and for others. What we are is formed out of the world we share with other human beings (Copeland, 1994: 135).

In one of his articles, Chappell wrote:

"Look at the underlying worldview of the age for educated people. That worldview is scientific, technological, mechanistic, positivistic, and secular. It has affected preachers and laity. It pervades Western civilization.

"It shot down a literal Bible, along with the threat of hell, the lure of heaven, a burning sense of sin, and fear as a powerful motivation toward faith and the church. (Dietrich) Bonhoeffer put it clearly 50 years ago when he wondered how to be Christian in a secular age, to which I add, 'and be honest.' The poet stated it powerfully, 'The center will not hold.' The net result is that we cannot threaten or scare educated people into church" (Chappell 1987).

Many people do not realize that fundamentalism, with its theory about a verbally inspired Bible, appeared rather late in Christian history. Martin Luther believed in the authority of the Bible but would not have shared the fundamentalist view of it: he questioned the inclusion of the Book of Revelation and was critical of the Book of James. To counter the Roman Catholic view of the authority of the pope, some Protestants proposed an inerrant Bible. Fundamentalism as a formal theology was not introduced until the early 20th century.

What the fundamentalist faith led to was walls, division, factions. It stressed laws, rules, demands, and exclusions. Its logic led to shunning, banning, to creating molds. It encouraged witch hunts, heresy wars, and hit lists. Those who didn't see everything the way "I" saw it were out. It was exclusive: only Christians, and only Christians who saw things a certain way, were accepted.

In place of this narrow faith, Chappell embraced a theology that was experiential: "I know when I bump into it in the midst of life." Life and faith itself are a process, an encountering of truth. Theology is a "doing." Truth comes to one in flashes or intuitive insights, what the Church has called revelation. Theology must be rooted in events that have meaning; it is something that reaches out and grabs us. It emphasizes self-understanding—what it means to be a human being. The human self is continually becoming; my self is part of an encompassing whole.

This approach recognizes the importance of the metaphoric and symbolic; in fact, all religious language is metaphoric. The symbol isn't the real. It's not the stuff we say about belief that embodies the mystery only pointed to. This approach leads us to make a fresh interpretation of the ancient revelations. Such a faith is historically aware, and appreciates the best of comparative studies.

The late theologian Albert Outler described what he called the quadrilateral, which recognizes four types of authority: Scripture, tradition, reason, and experience. Chappell believes that the four bases must be held in a dynamic tension to make sound doctrine. If we violate any one of these bases, we warp or deny some aspect of sound theology (Outler 1991).

Something that might be found in Scripture (especially something found in only a few verses) and practiced in tradition might be overturned by our reason and experience.

Chappell claims to have no favorite theologian, though he leans towards Paul Tillich (1948), Charles Hartshorne, Shubert Ogden, and John Wesley. "I do not think of myself as a theologian, but as a working pastor who strives to make sense of the Christian Faith." He is not completely comfortable with abstract thought and considers himself a reactive, rather than an original or systematic thinker. "I have long thought of myself as a sort of missionary to the 'cultured despisers of religion,' and I am also the mission field."

Some moderns have problems with prayer. Is there a God who hears, or much less answers, our muttered musings of instructions? Chappell feels the major problem saying prayers is simply taking time to prove the value. The proof is in the praying. Prayer comes *after* faith, and not before. Prayer, then, is a *response* to that which God has wrought. And if God has placed other people on our conscience, why not pray for them? Prayer is not a way to make God do our will. "I pray because I must, not because I've answered doubt with rational explanation."

What could be called progressive Christianity leads to love, grace, trust, justice, righteousness, mercy, kindness and hospitality. It liberates us from being bound to any formulation(s) of the past. We interpret the creeds in terms of what they were trying to clarify in their time and place regarding their encounter with the Holy. This leads to community, health, wholeness, openness, and joy. Rather than being exclusive, it is universalist: there are truths in other religions, and somehow God will find a way home for all his children.

When asked about death and what comes afterwards, Chappell replies that what is *going* to be is what *ought* to be in the wisdom of God. We have no certainty about the afterlife: we live by radical trust. There is a Power beyond the grave. Our religious language is metaphorical. The quest of religion is to encounter what is real behind the metaphors. The future is not in our hands: we trust God.

Chappell has no idea if he will see his parents again. In some parts of Scripture there is knowing and recognition—in other parts, extinction. Some passages suggest a kind of purgatory, and the longer Chappell lives, the more sense this idea makes to him.

In a letter (2004) to an inquiring friend, Chappell wrote, "I cannot imagine that the loving God addressed as 'Poppa' would forever damn any of his children because they did this or that, or didn't do this or that. Purgatory makes more sense to me the older I get, so God's love can work on after this frame turns to dust. I cannot imagine eternity, whether bless or terror…Maybe it would be more appropriate to remain only in the silent memory of God. I am fairly certain that my wish-thoughts do not project what is to be. So maybe it is better for me to simply leave all that to the wisdom of God."

A terrifying hell has no meaning (nor does a physical heaven). Chappell believes that God will not trash his creatures forever. When does a loving God stop loving us? The theologian Nels Ferre used to say, "God has no permanent problem children." (Though he does not stress this term, Chappell clearly follows Karl Barth and other theologians in favoring a kind of universalism, or eventual salvation for all.)

Socially and politically, such a faith respects all people, regardless of their nationality or race, and seeks to promote a peaceful, harmonious world. It avoids the idolatry of any specific economic system, and refuses to bow down to opulence and wealth. In keeping with Scriptures, it makes a special effort to identify with the poor, the downtrodden, and the forsaken. It is concerned about protection for our air, land, rivers, and oceans.

While this may be interpreted as a liberal faith, it does not conform to preconceptions. Wally's faith has become more biblical and more Wesleyan over time. The broad themes of the Bible are as relevant today as they were centuries ago. Chappell respects John Wesley's Christ-centered faith that was not narrow, and one that reached out to others who might disagree on some things.

"I stick to the faith and the church because it makes more sense to me for universal human and humane life style than any other; *and,* because something deep within kept calling me to it. That I identify with Wesley's 'assurance.' Such experiences bring their own verification.

"Lord, I am aware of your presence in the world. Where love is, there God is, and justice, truth, and mercy.

"Lord, I have warm regard for all persons at all times, and I work for justice, love, and fulfillment for all."

Chapter 6: The Board of Education

A Methodist minister is not employed directly by the congregation he or she serves, nor is he a member of that church. He or she joins an Annual Conference, a particular structure encompassing an entire state or segment of a state. Then the bishop—the highest official in the church—appoints (assigns) each minister to a congregation or to another position, such as hospital chaplain, on an annual basis, usually in June. Sometimes an appointment is made in the middle of the year because of an unforeseen circumstance, such as the death or sudden retirement of a minister.

When an opening occurred at St. Luke's Methodist Church, Dallas, in October of 1950, Chappell was named to serve this church. St. Luke's was the largest church any of his classmates was serving. Was this simply a fortuitous event, or did this mean he had the potential to be a real leader in his denomination? At one time he began to think it was not a question of *if* he would become a bishop, but *when?* But upon reflection he realized that, in a sense, he knew little about himself and little about the Methodist system. (More than once he was told, "You are the best bishop we never elected.")

He started out at this church like a whirlwind, yet 20 months later he accepted a move to another church. Reflecting on this, he wondered why he agreed to leave: Was he running away from work pressure? Was he trying to escape something in human relationships? Or did he feel drawn to his main interest of Christian education? He was not sure of the answer himself.

The minister at Floral Heights Methodist Church in Wichita Falls, Texas, was looking for an associate minister, and Chappell was named. He accepted this with the understanding he would be working in Christian education; he discovered that the senior pastor intended for him to do evangelism, which (in this case) meant ringing doorbells. Further, it appeared the senior pastor felt Chappell couldn't do anything right.

A Methodist minister is usually allowed to live in a house, known as a parsonage, for the duration of his appointment to that church. At the Wichita Falls Church, the house he and Stell had to live in was a little cracker box with no air-conditioning. (They finally got a small window unit.) This may have been the most frustrating situation the Chappell's had during his entire ministry.

Wally and Stell had been in Wichita Falls only four months when he was invited to join the General Board of Education in Nashville, Tennessee. This would have given him significant influence in Methodism in the fields of youth and recreation. While tempted, Chappell felt it was not right for him to leave his responsibilities so soon. But when another month passed and the situation at this church did not improve, he called the board to see if the position were still open. It was and he accepted.

They moved on December 1, 1952, and bought their first home in Nashville. Here at the heart of American Methodism a different world opened. The meetings, writing, travel, and contacts with some of the key leaders of the church were stimulating and broadening.

Prior to World War II, the guiding concept in adult education was that a teacher or leader would lecture or otherwise impart information to students, who would learn in more or less a passive manner. Another idea, begun at Bethel, Maine, was that the adult decides what he or she wants to learn in a class and the leaders serve as a consulting team to help him or her achieve this goal. This became part of a revolution in adult education, both in and outside of the church.

His responsibility on the board was for the older youth in the church, and his specific area was Christian fellowship, which included church recreation. He came to see that it is important that people think through the reasons they do what they do. The philosophy of recreation was deepened from simply "play" to examining the place of leisure in life. People need leisure in order to have time to reflect. A book that influenced Chappell was *Leisure, Basis of Culture* (Pieper, 1957).

This position required much writing including the editing of songbooks and a newsletter, preparing guidance materials for backpacking, one of his lifelong loves, and publishing a manual on folk dancing (with R. Harold Hipps). Chappell and Hipps published six more records in the folk dance series. His role on the dance manual was to make the instructions clear by using a glossary of terms and sketches of figures. For 30 years or more this was the best set of instructions available. He made important contributions to the curriculum at both the Methodist Church level and the National Council of Churches level. At the NCC, texts were selected and refined by the denominations and sent to writers to finalize.

Always an outdoorsman, Chappell began a long experience in mountain climbing and backpacking. His experience in backpacking in Colorado in 1956 with the Church of the Brethren was the first of 20 such adventures.

The opportunity in Nashville gave Chappell the chance to do extensive speaking and traveling, visiting every area of the country except New England and Michigan. He went to the position as a rather provincial Texas pastor; six years later he returned to Texas a citizen of the world.

He and Stell also returned with two more sons: Donald Edwin was born in 1952 and Lloyd James in 1954. Thus they had four sons, each born in an even year and born two years apart.

In 1958 Chappell returned to the North Texas Conference as pastor of Ridgewood Park, Dallas, only two miles from SMU. The church was four years old and had only about 350 members, but this was a talented and remarkable group of young adults. Their ability and commitment was well above average, and the church seemed on the cutting edge of movements in the church and in the country.

C. Emory Burton

Stell remembers Ridgewood Park as "our landmark church." She recalls that every Christmas members sent them Christmas cards with money in each one. The Ridgewood Park members were caring, creative, exciting people, and showed great interest in the Chappell boys.

In 1962 Chappell had the opportunity of leading a European tour. This would be the first of six such tours he would lead over the next 39 years.

Chappell recalls some wonderful times traveling to Colorado and California when all four boys were growing up. Yet their sons were entering their teen years during a turbulent era, and common teen-age rebellion did not bypass them.

Times were not easy, especially when the decade of the 1960s arrived. The civil rights movement was the dominant issue of the time, with somewhat uneasy support from the white churches, and much of the ambivalence was in the South. Many from colleges, churches, and the general population were protesting the war in Vietnam; women's rights, student rights, and environmental concerns were all in the news.

In 1963 when John Kennedy was shot, there seemed to be an evil spirit in Dallas. A local newspaper ran anti-Kennedy ads the very day he was shot. Lyndon Johnson and Adlai Stevenson were spat on during trips to the city. Once a newspaper boy came to the Chappells' door and asked Stell, "Are you all really communists?"

Chappell had several friends in the ministry who shared his progressive outlook, his idealism, and his questions about the direction of the denomination. One of their concerns was for racial justice in Dallas. They looked for justice in the public schools and prophetic preaching in their churches. Those who shared these concerns became known as "Renewalists." These friends decided to get together and form a study group, starting by looking at books, that would meet every two weeks—a group that would become enormously important in Chappell's life. At the meetings one of the members would bring a prepared paper describing his "pilgrimage." Each time the papers became more honest and complete, resulting in a great sense of relief, camaraderie, and binding.

They invited professors from Perkins School of Theology to stretch them beyond themselves. One of the people to speak to their group was Frank Littell, who had gone to Germany after World War II to help the church and developed lay academies there. These were ecumenical retreat centers that helped restore vitality to Protestant Christianity.

According to a history of the North Texas Conference, these young ministers banded together in "institutional frustration" causing them to "fight to love the church enough to stay in the ministry. One of the members, Jake Shelley, commented "All they can do is move you. They can't hurt you" (Hares, 2000: 99).

Meeting with this group, according to Chappell, was a major deepening of his identity and pilgrimage. It may have anticipated the emphasis in the church of small group, "koinonia" fellowship that stressed honesty, openness, and sharing. Members came to see they were not alone in their concerns, or as one member put it somewhat bluntly, "You knew you're not the only sonofabitch in the ministry."

The group was facing up to the humanity of the church. In one discussion, when they had detailed some of the compromises the church had been a part of, one member said, "It's like learning your mother is a whore."

"Yes," replied another, "but she's still my mother."

Some called this group the dirty dozen, because of the suspicion they aroused in the more conventional wing of the church. The taunt became a proud title. Chappell quipped, "We always laughed that any group would fear us, because we couldn't agree 100 percent on anything!" (Hares, 2000: 100). Members of the group, when interviewed many years later, considered this fellowship one that helped lead the church into honesty and relevance.

Renewalists grew from 12 to more than 100 and needed more space than Chappell's hospitality had to offer. They took their name but not their total agenda from a nationwide movement called "Methodists for Church Renewal" which was founded in 1963 in Detroit. One of their concerns was whom to support for election to General and Jurisdictional conferences: the group tried to support those with the same concerns for racial justice and church life. By the 1980s Chappell and Wilfred Bailey, a member of the Renewal group, were elected to represent the North Texas Annual Conference., and in 1988 Chappell himself along with others from this group were supported and elected.

(The General Conference, which meets every four years, is the highest structure in the United Methodist Church, and it and it only can speak for the denomination. It consists of 50 percent ministers and 50 percent laymen, who are elected from their respective areas as delegates. A point of interest is that bishops, the highest officials in the church, cannot vote at the General Conference and can address the conference only when given permission.)

Brian Forrester recalls with fondness his membership in the "dirty dozen" when Chappell was a senior member. Another member of that group, Patrick Hudson, was impressed with this talented group of Methodist clergymen, and adds that he learned a lot from them. In particular, he recalls Chappell as one with excellent people oriented skills.

"I have admired Wally from those early days in the dirty dozen to this day. Wally set a good example for me as a young person and provided insight into effective leadership and relationships. He was serious when the situation demanded it and was willing to take a public stand when needed. On the other hand, at informal gatherings and parties he was funny, friendly and relaxed.

"Wally was and is a serious student of the Bible, theology and social issues without raising his understanding of these matters to a level of untouchable perfection. In other words, he was and is willing to hear the views and opinions of others. Wally's willingness to listen is one of the keys to his effective leadership. Further, I don't remember his ever talking down to me as the youngest member of the group, or anyone else. He was not only a good but a courteous listener.

"I have seen him use his sense of humor repeatedly in group settings to lower the temperature of heated discussions and thus keep the discussion on a constructive track. Wally is not only candid and straightforward, but unfailingly civil."

A Christian Faith and Life community sprang up in Austin, dealing with religion and society, which was to become the Ecumenical Institute. The charismatic Joe Mathews, who had taught at Perkins, came to be the leader. Chappell and other participants, commuting from Dallas and other locations, would read papers and engage in stimulating discussions—even arguments--for three days a month for a total of four months. This gave Chappell a deeper understanding of theology and its relevance to the times.

The problem was that the Methodist Church was oriented around fellowship, doing good, and a simple theology. Most of its members were not ready for the more radical thought of the Ecumenical Institute.

The Ridgewood Park Church had moved from about 350 members to 550 or 600, including many gifted young adults. It was inevitable that a progressive minister would find opposition in his church, especially in a conservative area such as Dallas in the 1960s. Chappell had been involved in many activities outside the church, which caused resentment among a few laymen.

While a majority of the church did not want to change pastors in 1965, there were three ultra-conservative members of the Pastoral Relations (now called the Pastor-Parish) committee who desired a change. At one of their meetings, two of the seven members were absent, and the remaining five voted three to two for him to move. One member immediately called the district superintendent with this news, which meant that Chappell had gone onto a moving list before he had a chance to object.

Having spent seven years in a sophisticated church, Chappell was unprepared to be sent to Edge Park, a church in a different conference on the south side of Fort Worth. This church was only nine years old and had been served all this time by a man who was excellent in organization and personal relationships, but held to a conservative, revivalist theology. That proved to be a poor match for Wally and it did not work.

That year turned out to be a time when Chappell did his best to present an honest, progressive Christian faith to people who were not prepared for it. Since some conservative laymen liked to sing from old hymn books with gospel songs, there was some objection that Chappell preferred The Methodist Hymnal. He moved the following year and has never been back in that building. The district superintendent, who would have preferred to have another person come to that church anyway, did not lift

C. Emory Burton

a finger to help. (It is interesting that the following two pastors lasted only a year each.)

In February of 1971 Chappell wrote a poem, "My Vibes Are Out of Sync," which is worth quoting here:

> It is an odd sensation
> to feel oneself
> as out of step
> not only with his fellow preachers
> but with the Conference as well.
> Odd because my shape of self
> and central thought
> were molded in the church!
> Who drifted off from whom?
> And is there cause for worry
> deeper than to note the gap?
>
> It's easy flattery of self
> to say that I have grown
> with changing times
> to more contemporary lines
> at faster pace than church
> and most of preachers,
> though honest candor
> leans to that opinion!
> Maybe I have always marched
> a trifle out of step
> because my rearing led me
> from my youth to different view?
> I think that's true.
> My childhood church was not
> typical, but liberal,
> with heavy stress on education.
> Early we were liberated
> from a literal view,
> and early taught
> to mix the mind and heart
> in balanced portions,
> and leaven both with Scripture.

My home was pious Methodist,
though college-trained and thoughtful.

Maybe this disparity
(twixt me and some preachers)
is nothing but the broad plurality
of Methodism,
which holds a multitude of views
within one fellowship,
at least in theory.
Whatever is the cause and moment,
when I have spent a day
among assembled pastor types
I come away aware
my vibes are out of sync.

Good Lord, deliver me
from such conceit that treats
the problem oversimplified:
that everyone is out of step but me,
and those who stride beside.
But lead me, just the same, O God,
to confidence that you
have spoken truth to even me,
that I may stand in humble confidence,
though there be few within my tribe.

Chappell's next appointment would prove to be the most challenging and dramatic of his career.

Chapter 7: Surviving a Crisis

Georgetown United Methodist Church is located in a pleasant town north of Austin, the state capital. It is the site of Methodist-related Southwestern University. The school is a quality one but somewhat provincial. Chappell's appointment to this church proved to be an interesting and exciting one, yet the source of a major crisis.

The county judge, the president of the university, college professors, certified public accountants, and car dealers in the town were mostly Methodists and attended the church. Chappell, with his intellectual interests and cosmopolitan outlook, was an effective minister for the church, and in general he and Stell were well received.

For the first time in his ministry, Chappell began to preach from the lectionary. This means that one uses selected Biblical texts as they are proposed for each Sunday. The advantages of this method are that it keeps the preacher in the Bible, one is compelled to preach on a variety of subjects, and one must do research. Messages were strong, Bible-based without being anachronistic, and thought-provoking.

Chappell began several creative programs, such as study groups on the Bible and contemporary issues. He had the opportunity to rewrite the manual on backpacking he had written earlier. In terms of preaching, visiting, counseling, and staying active in community relations, this may have been the high point of his ministerial career.

Preacher, Prophet, Poet

The crisis came in his fourth year there. One son had trouble fitting into the conservative expectations of a Texas town. This was still the 1960s with its emphasis on freedom and youth rebellion. This son had long hair which was viewed with suspicion at that time. He played football the first year, but quit the team after a disagreement with the coaching staff, and was harassed severely.

One day in October, the Chappell family was relaxing and talking when the doorbell rang. Stell went to the door and was shocked to see two policemen. After flashing a search warrant, they burst into the home, asking "Where is his room?" Within a few minutes they had the marijuana in hand. They told the frightened teenager he was under arrest, read him his rights, clamped on handcuffs and led him out the door to their car.

Of course Wally and Stell were stunned at what had happened. Their concern, certainly at first, was not for their reputation but for the well-being of their son. Chappell went down to the police station and discovered that they would not even accept his check to bail out his son. He had to arrange for one of the doctors in town to come and write a check for the young man to be released.

This was the first time anyone in Georgetown could remember when someone from an establishment family had been arrested for drugs. News of the incident spread rapidly. It was a devastating experience for Chappell. He recalls that people came out of the woodwork to kick him over this incident. As he walked down the street, people would cross to the other side to avoid speaking to him. Stell adds that it was the first time either of them had known shunning.

Chappell left town with the understanding that Dr. Durwood Fleming, president of the college, would preach that Sunday. Dr. Fleming had a sermon ready to use, but about 5:00 Sunday morning decided he had to preach something else. He then developed a message on reconciliation which proved to be the perfect message for the congregation at that time. (Chappell's version of this is that it "saved my tail.")

Even though this seems unbelievable today, there was some question as to whether Chappell would be allowed to remain at that church, or even in the ministry at all. Twenty years earlier, he probably would have been out. But Bishop Pope came down to meet with the Pastor-Parish committee and worked to stabilize the situation until the next Annual Conference in June. He told Chappell that if he moved now, he would be "unappointable" (meaning no church would take him). Fortunately, with the support of Dr. Fleming and a few other key individuals, he was allowed to stay until the Annual Conference.

Part of the agreement was that he had to apologize to the congregation, a difficult step to take. He pointed out that no pastor is fully worthy to preach; he finds grace from the congregation to *allow* him to preach. The whole experience made him more humble and more vulnerable. (He does add that attendance was great for a few weeks!)

In addition to this disconcerting experience, Chappell learned that he had ruffled some feathers of some in the congregation, especially the narrow-minded school district and coaching staff. Fortunately, the experience was not all negative: there were enough good friends to provide support. The college hired Stell in the development office which proved to be a healing experience. She, like her husband, had great appreciation for the support provided by Dr. Fleming. But she did not think the Methodist conference provided the backing it might have, and there seemed to be a gap between the two of them and the bishop.

Stell believes she learned many things from this experience. She found more worth and value in their children than she had realized. This son went on to marry and become a great father himself, caring and patient. Wally and Stell are very proud of him, as they are all of their children and grandchildren.

Fortunately, Chappell had always kept a relationship with bishops and district superintendents. In January, he was offered the position of state director of the Methodist Student Movement (MSM) in Texas, effective at the coming Annual Conference. Chappell did not particularly desire an administrative position, but when the bishop told him that this post was better than anything he could offer him, he accepted. After all, working with young people had been a major part of his experience at the Board of Education. He left Georgetown defeated and resentful, but his involvement with student activities turned out to be a highly positive experience.

The MSM had been changing over time. In the past, the director had raised money and ensured that each campus in the state had what was called a Wesley Foundation director. But no new campus units were anticipated, and there had been some talk about disbanding the whole thing. There was a strong suggestion that the position might be short-term, probably only for two years. "Don't buy a house" was the advice.

Wally did such a good job with the student movement he was able to stay in this position for six years, longer than the average church appointment. He liked being an ombudsman, an interpreter and defender of the movement, but was not comfortable with the building and fund-raising aspects.

The office of MSM had been moved to Dallas, with a modest office on Caruth Street. In 1972, sensing that the position would last for some time, Wally cashed in an insurance policy and bought his present house on Santa Anita Street in Dallas. This $25,000 purchase proved to be a wise investment.

A few years earlier, Wally had become involved in the human potential movement, with an emphasis on sensitivity training, which he highly appreciated. He could build on this background, add an emphasis on organizational development and consulting skills, and make a real contribution to the student movement in Texas. He now had time, a budget, and no constraints on Sunday responsibilities. The MSM would offer annual summer training on an ecumenical basis, with as many as 70 attending. Once they took two busloads of campus ministers to Cuernavaca to hear Ivan Illich give some lectures.

The student revolt of the 1960s has been misunderstood. Some still think of it as a hedonistic enjoyment of drugs and free sex. While this aspect was clearly present, the revolt reflected a profound dissatisfaction with a materialistic approach to life. The campus ministry was close to the leadership of the student movement. But the latter tended to be heard as anti-establishment (one student speaker, probably speaking for other students as well, remarked "I don't give a damn about the local church"). This meant that Chappell was left to put out the fires.

In September of 1973 Stell had to undergo a radical mastectomy. Wally commented on the courage she showed during this ordeal, and her speed of recovery was a testament to her courage, confidence, and hope. There was no hint of tears, remorse, resentment, or regret. Wally felt they were both sustained by grace and he gained an awesome new respect for her courage.

During this period he attended a conference on human relations skills at Colorado Springs that turned out to be a major breakthrough for his whole life. He had gone through three consecutive churches where he left under something of a cloud. He had been told at one time that he was unappointable. This led to inevitable self-doubt.

At the conference, Chappell found a group that knew how to listen, a characteristic he had never given much attention to. The Dean of Students at the host school began by opening up to the group the personal turmoil he was having with his family. Each participant shared his concerns with the group and the other members responded. When it was Wally's turn, he expressed his self-doubts, and the other members responded. They saw many things in him he didn't see: they told him what a great guy he was, tall, good-looking, a fine speaking voice, and the like.

Following the instructions of the leader, Chappell lay on the ground. Members of the group lifted him up, rocked him and set him back down, an experience that led to tears. The experience was purgative, healing, affirmative, and actually turned his life around. An impossible situation had become an astonishing gift. All his self-doubt was swept away by the experience with this group.

Thus Chappell learned self-discovery, forgiveness, and acceptance. The administrative job he didn't particularly want turned out to be a gift from God, and these were memorable years. He was now so much stronger and clearer. Eventually he became an effective leader of workshops on group skills and leadership skills.

By the sixth year as leader of the state student movement, he knew it would end. His main work this year became setting up the system to run itself, which was only partly successful. At the end of the year, the MSM system was shut down and Wally was appointed as pastor of the Cochran Chapel Church, Dallas. Once Chappell left this position, his involvement with student activities was pretty much behind him except for one or two speeches to a Wesley Foundation.

By 1976, there was no effective student movement in Texas Methodism. Chappell believes strongly that the decentralization of the church has had some negative effects on the denomination, leaving local churches relatively autonomous entities. His views on the church, crystallized through long experience serving large and small churches, serving on a national board, and serving the student movement, will be considered in the next chapter.

Chapter 8: Thoughts on the Church

The six years Chappell spent in Nashville with the Board of Education gave him an appreciation of the larger hierarchy of the Methodist Church. The denomination placed some of its most trained and competent leaders on the boards of the Church, and they exerted creative leadership for the denomination as a whole. Methodism has always been a connectional church, meaning its local churches are tightly bound to each other and receptive to leadership from above.

But eventually there was a reaction to the hierarchy. By the 1950s a certain antipathy surfaced towards "Nashville" (a symbol of the authority structure of Methodism). Some in the church were resentful of apportionments, the assigned amount each church is asked to give to the organizational and outreach efforts of the larger church. In the 1960s the boards of Peace, Christian Social Concerns, and Temperance were merged into the Board of Church and Society (a move which may have made sense, but the number of people connected with the boards was cut considerably). In 1968 the boards of Evangelism, Education, and Lay Activities were merged into a Board of Discipleship, which Chappell said was like tying wildcats together.

In a 1987 article, Chappell grants that the chopping of these boards may have been needed, but he adds, "I don't think we did it wisely, for the net result was a dramatic, sudden, devastating cessation of leadership training efforts that had flowed from those great, flawed boards. Eliminate leadership development, and you just do not develop those who know how to witness and teach" (Chappell 1987).

It seems obvious to Chappell that massive leadership development is called for at every level. We have to begin with "leaders of leaders" training. That calls for those who are experts in pedagogy and not just content. "The training we need must be the kind that brings us out with changed hearts and behaviors, not just altered thoughts." If 3,000 United Methodist pastors highly trained in church growth and with theological depth would spend a day a week with nearby churches, pastors, and laity, it would make a dramatic difference. But the training must move to a depth level of spirit where the Spirit takes hold.

"I am of the opinion that our reorganizations of the last 20 years have added to our decline. Let a denomination or a conference get itself consumed with rearranging the institutional furniture (boards, agencies, mergers, conflicting programs, etc.) and you have a people who are preoccupied. Preoccupied folks don't hustle (for) new members. When you are scrapping over turf, you are not in an inclusive frame of mind" (Chappell 1987).

Chappell adds that he is not opposed to mergers, reorganizations, and the like. His point is that reorganization divides attention; tampering with the structure distracts us.

The controversy over structure continues as conservative groups within and outside the church would like to eliminate several organizations within the United Methodist Church. Their ire is particularly aroused at the Board of Church and Society and the Women's Division of the church.

The Board of Church and Society seeks implementation of policy statements of the General Conference on social concerns. It takes leading roles in working for policies to protect the environment, bring debt relief to impoverished countries, curtail the death penalty, address the HIV/AIDS crisis, and improve public education. Their broad program includes education, advocacy, resources creation, and communications. Yet the Institute for Religion and Democracy (not a United Methodist organization) wants to shut down this important board. (Nowhere does IRD express any interest in combating poverty, fighting racism, securing health care for all citizens, or taking steps to slow global warming.) Eliminating the Board of Church and Society would end the United Methodist tradition of prophetic social witness (Howell, 2003: 68).

Power is a problem for the Church—we seem to distrust it. Yet Chappell believes that if we are to deal with massive modern ills we have no other choice than to come to terms with power. Our concern is not just with individual souls; we are all about God's Kingdom breaking open on earth. While we need safeguards as we move into ministry, we cannot forget that power shapes the world and faith must wield it.

The Women's Division of the United Methodist Church has close to one million members who give more than $20 million a year for mission (2002 figures). Women give untiring, imaginative energy to mission in Methodist churches. They frequently share with their churches news from the world church. They read and discuss study books that expand their grasp of mission. They help move their congregations into work with their neighbors, especially those in need. "Progressive social-justice advocacy based on biblical mandate has been a hallmark of the women's missionary movement since its inception" (Howell, 2003: 64).

Two conservative groups, *Good News* and *Renewal Women's Network (Renew)*, would like to dismantle the heart of women's ministry and leadership in the denomination. Mission would be much more narrowly defined only as offering personal salvation, thus abandoning advocacy efforts toward a more just society for all God's children.

Renew is critical of the Women's Division support of interfaith dialogue that seeks to bring understanding between faith groups. *Renew* would end such dialogue, shifting focus only to converting people to Christ (Howell, 2003: 62).

The conservative groups falsely claim the Women's Division is not fully accountable to the church. The division is a unit of the United Methodist General Board of Global Ministries under the General Conference. It is accountable to a board elected through United Methodist Women (Howell, 2003: 63).

Chappell believes the conservatives are afraid of the women because they cannot control them and wish to keep them subservient. He has an affinity for the women's division because his maternal grandmother was one of the organizers of what became the Women's Missionary Society in the 1890s.

Other organizations under attack by conservative opposition include the General Commission on the Status and Role of Women, which works to achieve the full and equal participation and responsibility of women in the church, and the Commission on Religion and Race, which challenges the church to a full and equal participation of the racial and ethnic constituency in the total life and mission of the church (Howell, 2003: 69-70).

Theologically, some conservatives in the Church are trying to force their views on the entire denomination. They are getting money from outside foundations to have their ideas implemented in the church. Some are suggesting that those who disagree with their views should leave the church. Chappell likes to cite John Wesley, who believed we might not think alike but we can love alike. It's difficult to do that if some people want us to leave. "How can I love someone who wants to run me out of the church?"

The ecumenical movement was one of the encouraging trends in the last century. Its main purpose was to emphasize that the things that we agree upon are more important than the things that divide us. It has led to a working together of different denominations and to a dialogue with other religions, in which all of us can attempt to learn as we talk with each other. Chappell has been an enthusiastic supporter of the ecumenical movement throughout his ministry. The alternative is a narrow "us versus them" mentality that leads to tension and division.

Despite his concerns about the church, Chappell remains hopeful. He sees the church as a progressive movement, honoring the best in our Christian tradition without being bound to obsolete ideas and practices of the past. He sees the church as an institution that encourages the potential in all of us, individually and socially.

"Frankly, I do not see us dying, statistics notwithstanding. Rather, I see us in a period of adjustment, letting *some things* die that were good for their day but their time is no more, and moving us toward a new era of practical, gospel-based, thoroughly modern, Spirit-powered commitment that will be appropriate for...the twenty-first century" (Chappell 1987).

Chapter 9: Cochran Chapel

In the United Methodist Church, a district superintendent is a minister who has administrative supervision over a specified area, called a district, within an Annual Conference. In a sense, he or she is the pastor for the ministers of that district. That person usually has considerable input into the appointment of ministers in that specific district. All the district superintendents, acting under the bishop, comprise a cabinet.

Since Chappell wanted to have a long-lasting ministry at the Cochran Chapel Church in Dallas, he told the district superintendent not to call him too soon about the possibility of moving to another church. Yet six months after arriving, he was asked to go as pastor of the First United Methodist Church of Duncanville (near Dallas), and later was also requested to go to the First United Methodist Church of Commerce (east of Dallas). Each time he replied that he would go wherever the bishop wished, but he preferred to stay where he was.

And stay he did, for a fruitful ministry of almost 13 years, roughly four times the average stay of a Methodist preacher. Although it was a battle to get new members due to strong competition from other large churches in the area, things went well at the church. Chappell provided vibrant preaching and the church had a strong program, especially in music and drama.

Humor was a steady companion for Chappell during his church experience. Once he stood up to preach and reminded the congregation he was preaching a series. "Last Sunday," he began, "we left off where Jesus had been baptized by Jordan in the john." He had no idea why laughter spread through the congregation, and received some good-natured kidding afterward.

Frank, Chappell's older brother, came back to Dallas following his retirement, and to Wally's surprise, he and his wife Eleanor affiliated with the Cochran Chapel Church instead of the downtown church where they had previously been active. Frank and Eleanor were most supportive of their younger brother and brought writing and acting talents to the congregation.

About this time the thought of becoming a district superintendent occurred to Chappell, much as the thought of becoming a bishop had appealed to him earlier. Upon reflection, he realized this may have been just ego hunger, as he had not examined his talents and gifts carefully to ascertain if this was an appropriate role for him.

During this pastorate, Chappell began to develop what he called affirmational prayers, and continued to write poetry. In 1977 he conducted Intentional Living Workshops, and led a journal workshop which would be the first of some 100 he would lead over the next 27 years. In 1980 he led workshops on church goal-setting and on burnout in the clergy. He was president of the Dallas Pastors Association, board chair of Contact Dallas, and president of the RESTART Board, an organization to help the unemployed find work. He brought the United Nations-Washington seminar to north Texas, and was a longtime member of Christian Educators Fellowship.

The Board of Ordained Ministry is a structure within Methodism that helps prepare and evaluate ministers. Chappell was given the assignment of working on ministerial evaluation for this organization, and began a major study. He concluded that evaluation is best done by the individual person (or pastor) in the context of his or her own goals. The best evaluation is a cycle in which one tells himself what he has done with respect to appropriate goals. Although such a plan is now being used by many organizations, it was rejected by the Methodist Board, who preferred that evaluation be done by the district superintendents.

In 1975 Chappell had his first experience with journaling workshops, in which participants are taught to write about their lives, and in 1977 he became an accredited journal consultant through Dialogue House, New York. The approach was developed by the late Ira Progoff, a New York psychologist (Progoff, 1975). Such a workshop could be utilized by a person of any persuasion, religious or secular. The content was not religion or psychology or philosophy but one's own life. The objective was to enable people to move smoothly through their lives, and for them to be aware of what is happening to them in the process.

Progoff once said, "The Intensive Journal process is our inner workshop, the place where we do the creative shaping of the artwork of our life." Use of this method helps give a person's life greater direction, vitality and purpose. The experience can help one connect to his or her emotions and experiences; gain insights about relationships, career, and health. The workshop will develop a foundation for future decisions, reduce stress, and enable one to work through transitions.

Participants would log in data, read it back to themselves, and get what are called feedback leads, suggestions as to what to do with that data. Most of the process is a dialogue script with a piece of one's life, perhaps a person, a project, or an event. This can be a way of digging into one's unconscious, that part of life that is below awareness. One learns to live in a listening mode, hearing "the God who speaks within my thoughts," as Chappell said. He believes this is a superb instrument for awakening awareness and discernment.

"The Intensive Journal process has taught me to be dialogic in my thought," says Chappell, "with all sorts of conversations running in my mind, and insights from the unconscious flowing continually. It keeps me 'up' and charged and anticipatory." He has been leading these for 27 years.

Dottie Dunnam, a layperson who participated in one of the journaling workshops, recalls that Chappell gave an overview of the method and its history and levels. "Wally was clear, experienced, casual, (and an) expert at making us feel comfortable." Sandy Martin, another person who has taken the workshop, is similarly appreciative.

About 1995, Gary Duke, a librarian at one of the colleges in Dallas, was experiencing depression related to personal problems.

He had heard that Chappell offered training in journaling, and called him to see if a workshop would be offered soon. (Duke was not a member of Chappell's church at that time.) Chappell noted that no journaling workshop was scheduled, but offered to take Duke through the workshop via telephone. Every Friday for the next two or three months, Duke participated in the journaling experience with Chappell by way of the telephone.

Two models of leadership Chappell likes to explain are the cowboy and ranch foreman. The cowboy might have 40 acres and 200 head of sheep. He is like the pastor of a church of some 200 members. He or she knows everybody by name, loves people, and serves as a pastor to the flock. The ranch foreman has 45,000 acres, 25 employees, cultivates large portions of the land, looks after the machinery, checks the markets, hires and fires workers. In effect, he is the CEO. This is a model for the pastor of a large church. He or she is the one who looks after the goals, objectives, and long-range projections for the church.

In many of his workshops, Chappell used progressive relaxation training, which involved tensing and relaxing muscle groups until the whole body in relaxed. With appropriate prompting, one relaxes the neck, shoulders, jaw, face, etc. This can lead to a peaceful feeling as tension drains out. Even today Chappell uses this technique to relax in his office, car, or wherever he may be.

The world of nature has always interested Chappell, and when a friend mentioned that he was raising live oak trees, Wally perked up his ears. He joined the Texas Association of Nurserymen around 1980 and went to workshops to learn more about the enterprise. He helped his son Don buy some land near San Marcos, Texas, and planted a number of oak trees. For a time this was a serious hobby, but when he retired he did not have the space necessary to develop the interest. (With no prompting, Chappell talked about raising trees for 20 minutes.)

By 1987 it became clear to the leaders of the Cochran Chapel Church that a building was needed if they were to further their mission. After some study, a building program was proposed, but as often happens with an ambitious program such as this, there was opposition. In an acrimonious meeting to vote on the proposal, some in the opposition made personal attacks on Chappell and the plan was rejected. Chappell stayed at Cochran Chapel in Dallas another two years, but at 68 he realized retirement was near.

Chapter 10: And the Walls Come Tumbling Down: a sermon

The date was July 20, 2003, and the setting was the First United Methodist Church of Dallas, Texas. The preacher for this Sunday was Wallace Chappell, the 83-year old associate minister of the church, and his message went as follows:

Our lesson, Ephesians 2: 11-22, is filled with quaint, first century language, and runs rather long, so permit a condensation:

"For (Christ) is our peace: in his flesh he has made both groups into one and has broken down the dividing wall....the hostility between us...to create one new humanity in place of two, (to) reconcile both groups to God in one body through the cross...that then you are no longer strangers and aliens, but you are citizens with the saints, and members of the household of God."

One of the great pronouncements of the latter 20th century was made by Ronald Reagan, late in his presidency, when he stood before the communist-built Berlin Wall (a monstrous symbol of the closed, prison-like, gray world of communism) and proclaimed to the head of the Soviet Politburo and to all history, "Mr. Gorbachev, tear down this wall!"

It may have been the old actor's greatest line, as we watched world communism collapsing from its internal contradictions. It wasn't long afterward that Gorbachev confided to General Colin Powell, then White House Military Adviser, visiting in the Kremlin, "General, you don't understand; you Americans are going to have to find yourselves a new enemy."

Preacher, Prophet, Poet

Sure enough, the Soviet Union collapsed, the Berlin Wall came down, and the wall between the USA and Russia is still crumbling and dissolving, thank God.

Coincidentally, Reagan's challenging words are close to the heart of what Paul wrote to the church at Ephesus in our epistle for today. I know, Ephesians is one of the disputed letters, but to my unscholarly ear it sounds like Paul, and it bears strong similarities to the Roman letter at the point I touch today. Both Ephesians and Romans reflect one of Paul's deepest agonies: his concern for Judaism in its rejection of Jesus as Messiah, the division between Jews and Gentile Christians.

Paul was a devout Jew in addition to being converted to follow Jesus. He saw no conflict, no division, between Gentile Christians and Jews, and Jesus as the fulfillment of the ancient Jewish Law. For Paul, in Christ the two groups were one. And by implication, all humans, all peoples, are one in the grace and providence of God. In Christ, the walls are down.

That's powerful stuff! So beautifully stated in Ephesians! Some scholars think Paul was quoting an early Christian hymn, so the words may already have been well-tested, and represent the views of many Christians. However that may be, Paul celebrates the oneness of all believers, for whom the walls have been torn down.

Of course Ronald Reagan made no pretense of being a Bible scholar. His gift was acting and politics. But he was on target that day in Berlin, and in harmony with a central Christian teaching. And he gave us anew **our** clear agenda for the 21st century: we Christians must say to the world at a thousand points: "Tear down this wall."

Never was the call more needed, more poignant, almost desperate, than today. In every direction, every religion, every nation, every people, the walls of separation are firmly fixed in place. The human race is tragically divided; suspicion and hostility rule; hatred runs to terrorism; and killing continues almost unchecked.

Walls: we are split in every conceivable way: north/south, east/west, rich/poor, straight/gay, Christian/Muslim, Sunni/Shiite, Catholic/Protestant, liberal/Pentecostal, mainline Methodist/

Good News people, progressive/orthodox, black/white, rural/urban, Muslim/Hindu, American/French, English/Irish, Arabs/Jews, management/labor, farmers/migrants, my language/yours, educated/unschooled, tall/short, pop/classical, fat/skinny, upper class/middle class, Democrat/Republican, dressed up/informal, recyclers/garbage makers, ecologists/polluters, smokers/abstainers, old/young, my country/all the rest.

Got the idea? So many walls, everywhere, universal. It would be ridiculous, silly, funny, if it were not so *tragic, dangerous, ominous, deadly*; and (by my theology) flat out sinful.

God weeps when God sees our divisions, our walls, our separation, and the horrifying results on his people from such barriers.

It makes me wonder: are our walls human nature? Are we **bound** to this vicious circle? Is it so deep, so old, so complex that we **have to be** suspicious of anyone "not like me?" Sometimes I wonder.

But if that were true, then the Christian view would be a deceitful lie, and Pogo would have had it right all the time, "We have met the enemy and he is us." I don't want to believe that is human nature! I will **not** believe that! I **must** take a Christian stance on human nature.

I **choose** to see, I **will** see: One God, One humanity, One language of love, One small planet, and One lifetime for each of us. No time for walls.

So, I cannot accept the walls without a try at pulling them down! I cannot accept the accompanying violence as God's plan for the earth! It couldn't have been intended this way at creation!

So I have to seek a cure, a prescription for the problem of walls, walls which I must see as sin. So what solutions are available?

One solution the world has been trying for a long time is just to knock enough heads to force the peace. This approach emerged in the Tigris-Euphrates Valley shortly before 5,000 years ago; perhaps also in the Nile Valley, the Indus Valley and the Yangtze Valley. But it is most clearly stated in the Marduk myth, the "Enuma Elish," and in the ancient annual celebration in old Babylon of Marduk's victory: **Good violence drives out bad violence, and keeps the peace.** Scholars refer to this as "redemptive violence," if that is

Preacher, Prophet, Poet

not a contradiction in terms: redemptive violence, **what the good guys do to control "them," the bad guys.** Do I have to paint a picture? Five thousand years? Tigris-Euphrates Valley? Where are our soldiers today? And this has been going on 5,000 years? Am I missing something? And we are going to correct this in a few more months?

I suppose I am a bleeding heart Christian. If so, I'll wear the badge with honor. Listen to me: we bleeding heart Christians have to be realistic here, and give the devil his due: enforced peace may be better than endless violence with constant wall-building. Let me illustrate.

You older heads remember the Spanish Civil War of the 1930s. You younger heads perhaps have seen the movie, "For Whom the Bell Tolls," from the book by Ernest Hemingway, with Ingrid Bergman and Gary Cooper. **That** civil war. It was actually only the last of centuries of civil war in Spain between city-states: Leon, Castile, Catalonia, Toledo, Cordoba, etc. It finally came down in the 1930s to General Francisco Franco against the communists, and Franco Won, became a dictator, and severely suppressed all dissident factions for 40 years, the first extended Spanish peace in centuries.

As Franco neared death, an amazing thing happened: the leaders of all segments of society gathered to plan the future: leaders from banking, the military, business, labor, education, industry, even tourism. They solemnly agreed they would never go back to the days of in-fighting. And the modern economic miracle of Spain began. In Paul's language, they took down the walls.

When we humans are so consumed by hatred and violence, or greed and conquest, driven by religious fervor, it may be better to be forced to live together in peace; for then (perhaps) we can learn that those different guys are more like us, with wives and children, jobs and homes, just trying to make a living, and there is no future in killing each other. They took down some walls, ending the head knocking.

But there is a better way than knocking heads: the way of Christ, the way of love, One God, One humanity, One language of love, All persons precious in God's sight, and Universal commitment to peace.

Sounds good! How do we bring it off? How do we tear down the walls? Three short suggestions.

First, we must catch the vision. If you think I am sounding like an old revivalist, "Give your life to Christ," you're exactly right. Decide that you will live by Jesus' vision.

We will never tear down walls until we decide to. We will never get over our suspicion of someone "not like me" until we decide to. Walls are too deeply a part of human sin (as if it is genetic) to ever fall by their own weight. This is part of what theology calls "original sin."

So we begin with commitment to Christ, because our walls are largely invisible: we don't see them as man-made constructs. If we see them at all we think they are just the way things are! They will never come down until we make the commitment to tear them down, a commitment to a whole new life style. Give your life to Christ. Commit to living without walls.

Second, you have to learn to see the walls within yourself, which isn't easy. We easily deceive ourselves. I said that walls are mostly invisible. Unawares, we actively maintain them.

For many years I lived with a strong commitment to equality of the sexes, which doubtless began with a very strong and capable mother. For six of my adult years, in my thirties, I was part of the Youth Department Staff of the old General Board of Education of the Methodist Church. Of the 14 members of that the Youth Department staff, five were highly skilled, capable, competent women. I thought male chauvinism was behind me. Then about 18 years ago I was part of a pastors' study group that included two women pastors, and I made a horrifying discovery, through humor and jokes, that there was a residue in me of male superiority. A shock, and a shame--most humbling. What I learned is that there are walls in us with layers under layers, and often completely invisible.

So we have to watch our behavior for clues: really hear what we say and think; note from whom you divert your eyes, and note when the little meter in your head goes "Tilt!"

What does that for you?

Orange spike hair, black lipstick and body piercings? Dirty, ragged clothing and offensive body odor? Funny cars, or some with

Preacher, Prophet, Poet

all doors a different color? Weird haircuts? Dialect? Accent? No English at all? Maybe turbans, burkhas, veils or dashikis? What is it for you?

I'm saying we have to watch what I'm calling the "Tilt Meter."

I suppose I had, for a kid growing up in the 1920s, on the edge of the SMU campus, two of the most enlightened parents around. Both preacher kids, both strong Methodists, college graduates, fine Christians. But I remember one "tilt" from 1932 as vividly as if it was yesterday. The Great Depression was settling in, and unemployed domestic servants came to the back door of suburban homes to inquire for employment. One day I answered a knock and a black woman was there asking for "the lady of the house." I went to where Mom was and said casually, "Mom, there's a Negro lady at the back door to see you." As my saintly mother went past me toward the rear of the house, as if she were correcting my grammar, she said matter-of-factly, "Son, we say **black woman and white lady**." Tilt! Wrong! My mom is wrong! went my 12-year old kid meter. Where did I get that? From Sunday School? I have no idea. But I knew, and my tilt meter told me. We have to learn to see the walls within us.

Make your commitment; increase your awareness, and third, **we confess and correct**. Christians **do something about what walls they see**, something specific.

You look everyone in the eye and treat them as persons, servants, waiters, clerks, all. You stop to listen to a panhandler, and look him in the eye. You break the invisible shield that keeps you from seeing persons. You monitor the jokes you tell, and the jokes you laugh at. You find a tactful way to let others know they are stepping on the toes of your values by what they say. You guard your own language, and don't shout at those you disagree with. You let the world know you are trying hard to tear down the walls that separate us. Simple correctives—better than head-knocking, for they move us toward oneness in Christ.

I didn't say it would be easy. But it isn't impossible. Jesus set the course, and Paul accurately described it. It begins with you and me.

C. Emory Burton

I hold in my hand a little flattened glass marble, stuck in a loop of scotch tape so you can see it. I got it at the recent Annual Conference session of North Texas Methodism, where we had a service of confession and reconciliation between the races. Why did we need that? Because after 40 years in the same structure we still have walls. There has not been a successful black pastor of a white church or a white pastor of a black church, in our years in one organization.

It was a powerful worship service: great preaching, good singing, and these little tear drops: that's what they are, the frozen tear drops of too many centuries of racial injustice, separation and indifference: Walls!! We were given one as we entered, and after the money collection, these were also collected, cleansed and consecrated, then returned to us as we left the sanctuary, to be carried always, to remember the dark past, to see the walls that remain, and to work for a new tomorrow, when there is One God, One human race, and one language of love...when the walls come tumbling down.

Chapter 11: Later Ministry

In the fall of 1988, when Lomas Mortgage Company was looking for a vice-president for community relations, Jess Hay, who had been an active layman in Chappell's church, suggested Wally. At first, Chappell did not see himself in that role. He had always been a preacher, and he was not sure how he would handle a basically secular position.

But after some reflection, Chappell accepted the offer from the Lomas Company, beginning the work in February 1989. Since there was no job description, he had to determine for himself how a corporation should relate to the community. His counseling and organizational skills developed in the pastorate were useful to the company. There were two suicides in the company while he was there, and Chappell held both memorial services.

In 1990 the Chappells celebrated their 45th wedding anniversary, prompting Chappell to write a poem. He mentioned the jam-packed years, the personal problems that forced them to stretch and grow, all the shared experiences, travel, and friends. He then penned these words:

> But best of all
> my soul's companion
> of the way,
> the dearest one of all
> to me:
> so capable and energetic
> so real a person

C. Emory Burton

so beautiful
of body face and heart
so strong and poised
so steady in a clutch
so level headed, useful
with skills of tact
and confrontation keeping
me more human, selfless
    and effective.
I cannot even think myself
to milepost forty five
without her radiant presence
on the way.

Nor could I conceive
the journey on from here
unless she were along.

We've grown together;
at times through tears,
and other times through icy days,
again in roaring laughter.
But ever slowly,
step by step,
two forward and one back,
we've grown together.
The steady gaze
The lighter touch
The freeing spaces
in togetherness
Bodies uninhibited
Spirituality deeper
even than our prayers,
to love enough
to give each other
into God's own keeping
and live beyond
the ordinary fret of life.

> To know a deeply
> mystic comfort zone
> defying all attempt at words.
> We've grown together while
> we've grown alone as well.
>
> I can't believe
> it's forty five.
> Only yesterday
> she walked the aisle
> in white
> to join my hand
> > and vow
> > and life.
> It really seems
> forever.
>
> And is so satisfying
> > here today
> reflecting back.

The couple celebrated their Golden Anniversary in 1995 and anticipates their 60th anniversary in 2005.

One of the first churches he and Stell visited on retirement was the First United Methodist Church of Dallas. The senior minister, Hal Brady, had asked Stell to be a wedding consultant on several occasions, which gave them a tie to the church. They discovered the Aldersgate Sunday School class, a large, congenial fellowship where they felt quite at home.

In 1991 Chappell decided to attempt a bicycle ride to Gunnison, Colorado, to raise money for RESTART. He repeated the effort the following year, riding to and from Iowa City, Iowa. (See Chapter 12.)

When a well-liked woman in a previous congregation Chappell had served died, he was called back to perform the funeral service. After a meaningful ritual and a committal at the graveside, a brusque fellow grabbed Chappell by the lapel and said, "Wally, you old sonofabitch, you're going to die before I do, and you can't do my funeral? Can't you put something on tape?" (As it turned out, that man died several years later and Chappell came back to preach his funeral.)

When Lomas Company began to have financial difficulty in 1995, they offered Chappell a retirement package which he accepted. He assisted in the ministry at Walnut Hill United Methodist Church for a few months, and did the same at Southwood United Methodist Church in Oak Cliff (part of Dallas), a church served by a black woman pastor.

Wally and Stell had enjoyed their participation at the First United Methodist Church, and in 1996 Hal Brady invited Chappell to join their staff, working primarily in the areas of evangelism and visitation. About a year later, Brady returned to his native Georgia and John Fiedler came as the senior minister. A creative person and a fine administrator, Fiedler steered Chappell into the areas of endowment and pastoral care, responsibilities for which he was admirably suited.

By 1997 Chappell had serious problems with both knees. He had always been physically active and perhaps the years of mountain climbing and bike riding had taken their toll. After some consultation, he had two knee replacements on the same day, performed by two different surgeons. The replacements were successful and he was walking some the next day. After about a week of rehabilitation, he was getting around quite well.

Since total knee replacement is painful surgery, Chappell realized he would probably not have much of a prayer life, so he decided to deliberately lean on the prayers of his friends who came, using their words to penetrate the fog of pain and his racing imagery. He describes this as a powerful experience with a phenomenal outcome. "In these brief days of pain, drugs and mental confusion, 'the body of Christ' took on for me a physical (reality)...I was buoyed, sustained, inspired and defined, in awesome ways. The healing power of Christ was present in that hospital room."

Frank, Wally's older brother, had been in poor health for some time and died in February of 1998. What memories must have flowed as Wally remembered the youthful experiences with this brother, as he recalled how their careers took them separate ways and yet they were always bound together. Wally wrote a poem about his brother which is in the appendix.

For several months in 2003 and 2004, Chappell visited the federal women's prison in Fort Worth, working with the inmates in the area of journaling. The women included Catholics, Protestants, Jews, followers of eastern religions, and those with no religion at all. This study required three sessions of six hours a day. Some of the women responded well, but others lacked the cultural background. The project made Chappell aware of the lack of compassion our society has towards those considered deviant, with an emphasis only on vengeance and punishment.

All four of the Chappell sons live in Texas. While they are not active church people, they love their parents and have been fine husbands and fathers. Wally and Stell are blessed with eight grandchildren and one great-granddaughter.

Financing churches has not been an easy task in recent years, given inflation and an increasing indifference by many to the church. The cost of running a church, including maintaining property, paying for utilities and the like, continues to rise, so that much of the money goes for these things instead of for program. Chappell sought some creative ways to finance church expenses other than the routine giving of members, such as convincing some members of the importance of including the church in their wills.

In addition to working in finance, Chappell assisted in preaching, worship, the offering of prayers, hospital visitation, and leading workshops in such areas as journaling and in praying aloud.

One area where Chappell drew many favorable comments was in his pastoral prayers. It's easy for the minds of many in the congregation to wander off during the pastoral prayer, particularly when it consists of predictable clichés: "Teach us, O God, to follow thy will for our lives, and guide our nation in these troubled times." The fact that Chappell was a poet at heart led him to use the English language in a way that engaged the mind and enlivened the heart. (For a sampling of his prayers and poems, see appendix.)

John Fiedler, senior minister at the church, first met Chappell when he was hosting the *Faith Focus* television show in Dallas, interviewing Wally on his long bicycle journey to Colorado.

Although Chappell wore a crew cut that gave him the air of a military man, Fiedler soon realized that this man was a poet, a prophet, a theologian, and a pastor.

"When I came to First Church Dallas in the summer of 1997, Wally immediately made a beeline for me and told me that our covenant would be that as soon as I decided that he was no longer (effective) that I was to inform him and he would immediately step aside. Periodically, Wally has checked to make sure I haven't forgotten that arrangement but the truth is I have not forgotten. ...I simply have seen no sign of Wally's slipping at all. The only visible sign of aging is his walk. ...Periodically, I have asked Wally to slow down on hospital visitation, to no avail. He responds by saying that he loves it.

"Every day that Wally spends with our staff is a great gift. The joy is not only in listening to his wise comments and his great sense of humor but also in watching him have fun. Wally has said to me, "Chief, my entire career I've aligned myself with losing causes and here I feel like we're on to a winner." Even with his renaissance qualities, Wally has never tried to second guess my leadership or decision-making. He has always been supportive, helpful, and kind. I know that I speak for the entire staff when I say that we have a strong love and respect for this wonderful servant of God."

An associate minister at the church, Alexandra Robinson, says, "Besides generating a file folder titled "Wally" filled with articles he has offered to me over the years, he has given me a true understanding of what it means to be in a lifetime of ministry. As my husband says, 'When Wally speaks, it is like God's wisdom has come down.'

"I have never met anyone as passionate about the church, genuinely concerned about the wellbeing of others and positive about God's work in the world, as Wally Chappell. He has developed and molded his theology with the times, while taking a social and emotional stance for what he believes to be truth. If I am able to make a quarter of the difference that he has made in ministry, I will consider myself worthy of the honor of following him as an ordained elder in the United Methodist Church."

Dana Effler, director of music and arts at the church, writes:

Preacher, Prophet, Poet

"Wally Chappell amazes me! His insight, honesty, compassion, and depth of faith are truly inspirational and set a shining example. His openness, humor and progressive thinking make him a contemporary of every age group here at the church. We all love Wally and treasure every day we have with him.

"I can't think of a better goal for myself than to age as well as he has. He is 84 years old and still loves life and people, never ceases to find God in every day, and continues to lead a productive, grace-filled life. Thanks be to God for Wally Chappell!"

Pat Beghtl-Mahle, a district superintendent in Texas, speaks warmly of Chappell. She recalls that he was her minister when she decided to enter the ministry, and she served as an associate minister when Chappell was at Cochran Chapel. She claims that he has an outstanding sense of ministry and ability to relate to people. In addition, he is always working for improvement. "I am amazed and grateful for his guidance."

As of 2005 Chappell will have served 60 years in the ministry of the United Methodist Church. He continues not only to influence others by his ministry, his prayers, his poetry, and his workshops, but he continues to read, to study, to audit courses at Perkins School of Theology, to grow. "I am a much unfinished piece of work, very dependent on grace and guidance."

Chapter 12: Colorado and Back

By 1991 Chappell had become involved with RESTART, an organization seeking to get the unemployed back to work in lasting fashion. After two years as secretary of RESTART he became Chair, having to confront budget deficits, find new board members, support the staff, and build bridges.

Raising funds is seldom an easy or exciting undertaking. There were staff salaries to be paid, client food to buy, and mortgage payments, among other expenses. Could there be a way to give publicity to the fine work RESTART was doing and raise funds at the same time? One day he heard the term "Charity Ride" applied to bicycle trips. If he and others could find sponsors for a bicycle ride to Gunnison, Colorado, and attract media attention, they would achieve publicity and raise money.

But he was 71 years old! A knee had blown out when he was 57, ending his handball career. Would he be able to bicycle some eight hundred miles? Although he had been riding his exercycle faithfully for the last four years, he had never attempted anything like this. It took conversations with experienced bike riders, information on charity rides, cost estimates, time tables, and map study to complete the planning.

Chappell decided to take a friend, Bob Foster, who would drive a car to use when it was not feasible to go by bicycle. At the sendoff on June 7, many friends and more than 100 Lomas Company employees gathered for a brief ceremony and farewell.

Preacher, Prophet, Poet

How does one come to know with unbending certainty that one *must* do something, *can* do something, and *will* bring it off? As Chappell expressed it, "Whence stems that inner voice which seems to come from some strange ultimate beyond? What heavy cosmic hand is laid upon our shoulder impelling unforeseen and totally unexpected courses? How did I get here on this jaunt?"

Perhaps roots of the motivation lay in childhood: an active father who worked away at health, fitness, sports, and diet long before the recent fad. Parents, teachers, and youth conferences had formed in him an attitude that Christians put their deeds beside their creeds. And Chappell had always loved sports and tried to keep in shape.

In February he had sounded off in print and pulpit on the need for volunteers and voluntary giving as the only solution to a multitude of modern social ills. Now, he felt, he must do what he had been talking about. The inner vision shaped the outer action.

The trek was quite an adventure. When there were no vehicles passing, the wilderness along the roads was absolutely alive. Once two large birds with curved beaks the size of a pencil must have been disturbed that he was near their nest, for they paralleled him for 15 minutes, each off to one side, fussing all the way.

The smell of passing cattle trucks lingered long after they had passed. The stench of a passing garbage truck would finally be replaced by the smell of new-mown hay and fields of alfalfa. They passed an astonishing number of dead creatures, especially armadillos and turtles, as well as a million grasshoppers in two sizes and colors; honey bees, a wider variety of birds, more furry things of indescribable variety; several kinds of snakes, frogs, horned toads, mice, spiders, a skunk (easily identified!), a jackrabbit, a coyote, a hawk.

Chappell observed, "One gets the clear impression that one doesn't wish to join the ranks of the road kill. The fragility of all of life is clear. But if I have to go before my time, I'd rather do it on such a crazy jaunt than in a stupid traffic accident at home."

What a variety of trucks he saw: gas trucks, moving trucks, shipping trucks, pest control, UPS, welding rigs, farm trucks, syrup trucks, pickups full and empty, and more. Debris included dozens of broken bungee cords; tire parts, shock absorbers; lumps of mud; dozens of bolts from ½ inch to 6 inches; and all sorts of metal pieces.

Then there was the pain. Pain would come in his legs, his feet, his bottom, his wrists, the muscles in his upper arms. Uphill riding makes for hard breathing. Most of the hills could be negotiated by using all the gears, but one or two required walking up the last part, pushing the bike. The wind was unpredictable, sometimes gently aiding the ride, sometimes blowing hard in his face. He had to watch for traffic at all times, especially near freeways, and avoiding the trash, bumps, holes, ruts, and loose rock was a consuming task.

Chappell had sent out publicity to newspapers and TV stations and sometimes stopped along the way to publicize the effort. Once or twice the media outlet showed no interest, but usually Chappell and (Bob) Foster were well received.

Evenings in a motel were spent eating dinner, writing up a log of the day's events, making phone calls, and resting. His prayers were little but thanksgiving: for all the help in preparation, for the bike and the road, for Bob and the whole adventure.

On June 19 the trek came to an end with the arrival in Gunnison. The reception included friends and the mayor and a few curious onlookers. Chappell was awarded a Gunnison pin and patch for his jacket. He estimates that in the 13 days he traveled 770 bike miles, 67 ½ hours on the bike, 4,057 minutes less 115 minutes coasting downhill, and approximately 335,000 foot revolutions.

As Chappell reflected: "Led by the inner light, the voice of God, altruism, the pressures of necessity, or whatever you want to call it, what have I accomplished?" As the days permitted a perspective to emerge, he named these things:

He had raised more than $36,000 in cash and pledges for RESTART. He had proved to himself he could do it, and the adventure had not been all that dangerous, nor all that big a deal. The trip brought some great public relations for RESTART. The experience reinforced the importance of volunteering, taking action for one's beliefs, and for voluntary giving. It demonstrated that senior citizens can make a difference, and that individual efforts are significant. Chappell got himself in the best physical condition he had been in in years, and come back feeling strong, with his endurance and flexibility improved. The trip rallied quite a few people by a vision and even an inspiration.

"It enormously increased my appreciation for and love for God's created world in all its vastness, beauty and diversity. I discovered a deepened sense of gratitude for many good folks who helped in so many ways, both on the scientific side of all the gear, nutrition, training, etc.... of caring, interest, lodging, food and even laundry. I was grateful to God for accomplishment, safety, the love of dear ones and friends, and the opportunity for adventure; for life needs adventure."

A year later Chappell, then 72, completed another bike ride to Iowa City, Iowa, to raise money for RESTART. Early in the trek they had two days of rain and in northern Oklahoma, the temperature, with wind chill factor, was down to 41 degrees. "We came expecting summer," Chappell said. This time he was accompanied by Carrol Caddell, a Dallas Methodist preacher, and Chappell's nephew Philip Glenn, who ended his ride in Kansas City. They were on the road for 13 days and averaged about 70 miles a day.

Reflecting on the experience, Chappell wrote a short poem he called "Prayer Won't Pedal:"

> Out there touring
> on the highway shoulder
> there's one thing praying
> will not do:
> It will not push the pedals!
>
> Though God can help
> me *want* to keep
> on going, God doesn't
> do the pedaling!
> Though prayer may bring
> a sense of Blessed Grace:
> to be alive and on the road
> *at all*, and
> even lift one's spirits
> in the spinning,
> God doesn't push the pedals.

> Prayer changes everything
> except
> that we must do our living.

The main point was not the novelty of bike trips but the dramatization of volunteer service. Chappell said if people care about social problems they need to consider volunteering at least two hours a week. "It's got to be done by millions of individuals," he added.

Chapter 13: Reflections

Having lived through some turbulent times of the twentieth and early twenty-first centuries, Chappell has had an opportunity to reflect on some of the critical issues of the era.

World War II began when Chappell was 21 and the war in Iraq occurred when he was 83, and in between there were several other conflicts, including one in Korea, Vietnam and the terrorist attacks of September 11, 2001. It is not surprising that a minister who lived through this history would have strong views on war and violence.

Chappell bought into the pacifist views of Marshall Steel, the dynamic preacher at the Highland Park Methodist Church of Dallas. Is this not what Jesus taught, especially in the Sermon on the Mount, and in the way he lived his life? The writings of Harry Emerson Fosdick supplied a thoughtful foundation for a philosophy of nonviolence, and this was reinforced by the teachings of Dr. Martin Luther King, who was influenced by Gandhi.

And yet a pure pacifism seemed inadequate to deal with some harsh realities of a complex world, and Chappell was familiar with the anti-pacifist views of Reinhold Niebuhr. Was pacifism really a live option when Hitler was marching over Europe? Does not an organized society have the right to defend itself? Might there not be circumstances in which the application of force might do more good, or at least prevent more harm, than a hands-off policy?

Spain had been having periodic civil wars for hundreds of years when Franco, ruling with an iron hand, forced peace on the people. At his death, Spanish leaders from all the major sectors of life met and agreed not to resume the fighting. Then the modern economic miracle of Spain began.

While a defensive use of force could be rationalized, the emphasis of a Christian position must be on peaceful relations and nonviolent resistance. An obsession with military preparedness is not only expensive, but may blind us to more constructive approaches. Chappell thought the Vietnam War was foolish, based on a Messianic complex that we were going to save the world, though we had little idea of what we were doing. We were obsessed with Soviet communism, an oppressive system that fell of its own inherent flaws. Chappell recalls having the funeral for a fine young man killed in Vietnam and felt it was such a waste.

The tragedy of September 11th was a wakeup call for America. The following Sunday, September 16, Chappell spoke to about 200 people at the First United Methodist Church during the Sunday school hour. He pointed out the need to understand the thinking of Muslims who have felt oppressed for many years, and spoke of the folly of waging a war against Islam. He received no critical comments and had many requests for a copy of his statement.

Rene Girard (see Related Reading) had shown how some people can give a religious justification for oppression and dominance. A mythology emerged 5,000 years ago that claims we can use good violence to drive out the bad violence. Before 5,000 B.C., violence was sporadic, not carried out by standing armies, but in the last five millennia it has become "ritual violence," that which is institutionalized as part of the system.

Our response to September 11th, according to Chappell, was wrong-headed from the start. We went into Afghanistan and later Iraq with a cultural naiveté about these people. You can't kill ideas with guns, and our response may be creating more terrorism. We've made the Muslims angry with us, the Palestinians hate us, and Japan and some European countries dislike what we have done. What we must do is see each other as human beings.

There is no future in killing—violence begets violence. If our response is just to kill off the Muslims, we will have descended to the level of animals and Chappell would not want to live here. The ones to put a stop to terrorism may be the moderate Muslims.

In 1995 the Federal Building in Oklahoma City was bombed. In a dialogue script in his journal, Chappell was reacting to this terrible event and used a poem worth repeating here (in part):

> But what to do with perpetrators
> of monstrosities? And
> how eliminate what creates
> such a murderous rage?
> The nation cries the ancient
> cry for Abel's blood!
> Yet Jesus told me we
> could hang those guys
> and feel avenged,
> yet not affect at all
> the steady manufacturing
> of terrorists who hate
> so much they wreak their violence
> on strangers, devoid
> of conscience or remorse.
>
> He further called me
> to a new community
> (the Reign of God)
> of justice to the poor
> the castoff and the powerless,
> community that makes
> a human whole,
> that brings us face to face
> in dialogue-without-invective,
> in dialogue that alters economics,
> changes feelings, opens empathy,
> breeds possibility for worthy earnings
> respecting everyone, eliminating
> breeding grounds of violence.
>
> Much more we talked about.
> It was a life-transforming
> conversation there with Jesus,
> jotted in my notebook.

>   He reassured he'd always
>   be available.
>   I left with clear resolve
>   to help, some place
>   some kids, to stay in school,
>   to be productive, feeling useful,
>   outgrowing seeds of hatred.
>   Unless we do that
>   on a massive scale,
>   one kid—one mentor,
>   then hanging high
>   another crazy guy
>   won't do an ounce of good.
>   A hanging only proves the people, too,
>   can kill without remorse.

An added concern to the terrorism issue is the curb on our freedoms. The administration introduced serious infringements on our freedom and attached a high-sounding name to them: the Patriot Act

Chappell was involved in the civil rights movement, the number one domestic issue of the last century. He had friends who went to Selma, Alabama, for a voting rights demonstration in 1965. Later, he marched in downtown Dallas on this issue. He still considers race an important concern and continues to preach on the subject.

A movement on the right today opposes liberalism. A fiscal conservative, Chappell believes that society has responsibility for the poor and needy. He sees this as Christian and biblically based. Taking care of the weak is the only way we can survive. When schools are inadequate, young people see their lives ruined. The campaign to cut government services and starve the system is seriously misguided.

"We Democrats," says Chappell, "have been accused of throwing money at problems. But what the conservatives do is throw unproven, unhistoric theories at them, which will not work in the long run."

The cultural shift towards free markets concerns Chappell, not because he opposes a market economy but because of a false emphasis on accumulation of vast wealth and the stamping out of labor unions with little concern for the struggling worker. The high salaries of CEOs he considers immoral. He refers to a documentary that interviewed the children of immensely wealthy people who, lacking the experience of making it on their own, became withdrawn and distrustful.

According to a well-researched book Chappell recently read, within the most prosperous fifth of U. S. households, growth was shared so unevenly that some 90 percent of that fifth's gain went to the top one percent. The richest 2.7 million Americans, the top one percent, have as much after-tax dollars to spend as the bottom 100 million (Phillips, 2002: 103, 1999 figures). When I mentioned having seen a bumper sticker that read, "Jesus was a liberal," Chappell offered the view that Jesus was, in fact, a radical. "Sell all you have and give to the poor" (Luke 18: 22). He added that he knew a man who did just that: he recalls the sense of peace he felt when he gave away his last keys. He felt that he had not owned these things; they had owned him. This man took a small suitcase to Nicaragua to live on $25 a month as a village elder.

Ugly political campaigning, which seems to get worse rather than better, is a concern for Chappell. It is possible to disagree with people without attempting to destroy them.

When asked what books influenced him, Chappell began with Lloyd C. Douglas' *The Robe*, which he grants is not a great book but one which had a pivotal influence on him (see chapter 4). In later years, he was much influenced by the trilogy by Walter Wink, a definitive study of principalities and powers (Ephesians 6: 12), which Wink defines as the system or establishment.

According to Wink, movements for social change will simply never succeed unless they come to terms with the existence and pervasive presence of the structural and spiritual forces the Bible refers to as principalities and powers. These "powers" are institutions, structures, and systems, both spiritual and institutional.

"Violence is the ethos of our times. It is the spirituality of the modern world. It has been accorded the status of a religion, demanding from its devotees an absolute obedience to death." Wink believes that devotion to violence is a form of piety.

In the myth of redemptive violence, Wink continues, the survival and welfare of the nation are elevated as the highest earthly and heavenly good. According to this viewpoint, there can be no other gods before the nation.

This ideology gives the nation's imperialistic imperative divine sanction. By divine right the state has the power to order its citizens to sacrifice their lives to maintain the privileges enjoyed by the few. By divine decree it utilizes violence to cleanse the world of evil opponents who resist the nation's sway. Wealth and prosperity are the right of those who rule in such a state. And the name of God can be invoked as having specially blessed and favored the supremacy of the chosen nation and its ruling caste (Wink, 1992: 26).

This mythology uses the tradition, rites, customs, and symbols of Christianity in order to enhance the power of a wealthy elite and the goals of the nation narrowly defined. It has only casual interest in compassion for the poor, or for more equitable economic arrangements, or for the love of enemies. It uses the shell of religion intent on the preservation of privilege at all costs (Wink, 1992: 28).

Bernard Scott's *Hear Then the Parables* asks how the parables would have been heard in the culture of their time. Every one of the parables, observes Chappell, has to be re-thought. Imagine how the first hearers would have heard the parable of the workers in the vineyard, when all the workers were paid the same for different amounts of work.

Chappell is selective about movies, only going to those he is quite sure he will appreciate. Some he named include the classic *To Kill a Mockingbird*, as well as *Guess Who's Coming to Dinner, In the Heat of the Night, On Golden Pond, The Sting, The Apostle, The Sixth Sense,* and *O Brother Where Art Thou* (especially the music). He dislikes films with a major stress on organized crime and violence, and never saw *The Godfather* movies or "The Sopranos" on television. With so many impressionable people around, he feels these things need not be glorified.

Actors who impressed him include Spencer Tracy, Katharine Hepburn, Henry Fonda, Marlon Brando, Paul Newman, Robert Redford, Vanessa Redgrave, and Hal Holbrook. His favorite comedian was Jack Benny, and he thinks Lily Tomlin had some funny routines. He doesn't care for vulgar routines and thinks some comedians get pretty sick.

Most of the sitcoms on TV Chappell finds to be mindless diversions that are a waste of time. (But he does rationalize sports as a diversion.) He liked the old Western series, "Gunsmoke," and the TV series, "Lonesome Dove." He considered "All in the Family" to be groundbreaking, if not classic.

Growing up in the Big Band era, Chappell loved the music of Glenn Miller, as well as Tommy Dorsey and others of this type. On New Year's Eve in 2000 he and Stell danced the night away to a Glenn Miller orchestra in Iowa City, Iowa. (There were perhaps 300 people on stage as well as the orchestra.) By the age of 20 he was enjoying the operettas of the time such as *Naughty Marietta* and *The Student Prince*.

Lawrence Prehn, Chappell's college roommate, helped him learn to appreciate classical music, including Beethoven, Brahms, and Bach. He used to listen to classical records while studying, so that strains of melody fixed themselves in his mind. He adds that he could appreciate this music without much understanding. Rock music, especially the hip hop type, has no appeal to him whatever.

While jazz did not speak to Chappell at first, he learned to listen to it and makes an interesting comparison between jazz and preaching. In a way, he says, sermons are spoken jazz, a momentary creation. Jazz can build a momentary bridge between the musicians and the audience. When this connection occurs, it is a great moment. It is similar with preaching: the sermon is not found on paper—if it works, it is an electric connection, a happening.

In later years, Chappell's tastes moved more into hymnody, though he appreciated the message more than the music. He likes many of the great hymns of the church such as "All Hail the Power of Jesus' Name," "Morning Has Broken," "Hymn of Promise," and many of the Charles Wesley hymns. He considers himself an emotional, sentimental person, especially when hymns speak to him in a profound way.

His hobbies have included serious lawn care, gardening, casual woodworking, photography, jeeping the high country, swapping tales, teaching and preaching, playing grandpa, exercising for health, and travel.

He has been to Europe six times, Mexico three times, has made several trips to New York City, Chicago, St. Louis, Denver, San Francisco, Seattle, the Rockies and Smokies; he has seen a ball game in Yankee Stadium, cruised in the Caribbean and Hawaii, visited Key West for five days, made several major climbs, spent 20 years playing handball.

"What a rich, varied, interesting, stretching, challenging life. I really can't believe it."

On self-analysis, Chappell once wrote:

"I see myself as a humble man. I know I can do some things well, and am self-confident, always attempting anything. I also know that I've had a varied, long, interesting pilgrimage. But the sense of humility is there because I also know my weaknesses, limitations, mistakes, shortcomings, etc. Also I have known some truly great people and I am not in their ballpark intellectually, in capabilities, in saintliness, and selfless service. I know my weaknesses quite well—I work on them—I have made *some* progress—but I find what I dislike in myself is dastardly persisting. So humility comes easy. As the hymn says, 'Go spread your trophies at his feet, and crown *him* Lord of all.'"

Chapter 14: The God of the Mountains (a sermon)

A group of retired Methodist preachers gathered on October 8, 2003, for their regular meeting in Dallas, Texas. After a meal and some music, 83-year old Wally Chappell stood to speak. His sermon was entitled "The God of the Mountains."

This past June we went to Colorado to help scatter the ashes of the patriarch and matriarch of a family. That was the first time I had ever done anything like that—a scattering of the ashes ceremony at 10,500 feet elevation. The experience made me think of Jesus' transfiguration, which is also the regular text for Transfiguration Sunday in the Christian year.

Quoting from Matthew: "Six days later, Jesus took with him Peter, James, and John, and led them up into a high mountain apart by themselves. He was transfigured before them, and his clothes became dazzling white, which is like God. And there appeared to them Elijah and Moses, talking with Jesus. And Peter said to Jesus, 'Rabbi, it's good for us to be here; let us make three dwellings, one for you, and one for Moses, and one for Elijah.'" Then the gospel writer inserts this sentence, "he didn't know what to say, for they were terrified." Do you hear his voice cracking? Peter was so scared he had to say something.

Then a cloud overshadowed them, and a voice from the cloud said, "This is my son, the beloved, listen to him." Suddenly when they looked around, they saw no one with him any more, but only Jesus. The simple fact is that mountains and deserts have an amazing history in Judaism and in the Christian tradition. The same can be said for a group of Texans who hike off to Colorado every summer to see the beauty there and get away from the Texas heat. Many of us love Colorado and have for a long time. Like the old Hebrews, we don't just vacation—we have powerful encounters with the holy up there in the mountains.

About 30 years ago I was with a backpacking group in the high San Juans northeast of Durango about five miles into the wilderness area. We were on a circuit route; we left our old school bus at the last pass before you get to Silverton. From there the trail took us about five miles down to the Animas River, and from there up the Elk Creek Canyon.

In a wilderness area such as this, you don't measure distance by miles nearly so much as by hours. This back country is rough, wild, severe country, totally indifferent to human safety. More than once I have been scared half to death by experiences in the mountains. In the morning we hiked up Johnson Creek and I found myself hiking alone. The stronger campers had gone out early and were well ahead. Years before I had learned that when I have a long ascent, I do better with a slow, steady pace, slow enough to allow my oxygen to keep up. The higher you climb the shorter your steps, and the more breaths it takes per step to maintain your body's needs.

A strange thing happened that day that I did not understand. I began to have a conversation with the mountains, and they talked back to me. It was as if a strange yellow or orange light came over—I don't know if it was visible or simply in my head—and I had a conversation with my recently departed parents, and I also talked with God. I experienced a sense of the nearness of God; at times I wept unapologetically, I laughed out loud, talked out loud, and I felt myself overwhelmed by the goodness of life and the deep, abiding sense of blessedness. God was so close, a great feeling of bliss just took over my whole being, and I knew something unusual was happening, too vivid to be suspect, and it seemed to carry its own authentication.

Some years later, in reading up on altered states of consciousness, on meditation theory and practice, and a kind of prayer monks call contemplation, I learned about the effect of rhythmic breathing, where inhaling and exhaling were coordinated over a steady pace. I had approximated the same practice that monks and saints and mystics had learned over thousands of years. What this does is set the stage for the person to whom it happens, and one senses the nearness of the reality and love of God—the God whose holy mystery is at the heart of life—the God we cannot name but cannot doubt. It was for me like Moses' burning bush experience: so vivid, indescribable, convincing, and compelling. Years later I know that mountains and deserts can do that to us, something God's saints have known for a long time. It's no coincidence that monasteries and retreat centers have been founded in mountain and desert settings. For over 1,600 years heroic Christians turned to the wilderness, alone, out in fierce, hostile and dangerous terrain, to spend their lives in searching for God. Their writings became the prototype of monasticism and pioneered the deepest forms of prayer and communion with God.

Of course there were precedents in the Bible for mountains and an experience with God. God came to speak to Moses and Elijah on mountains. We recall the passage where God came to Elijah not in the wind, the earthquake, or the fire, but in a still, small voice, which in the Revised Standard Version reads, "the sound of sheer silence." God then sent him back to his work as a prophet.

In the Christian Bible, 850 years after Elijah, Jesus, following his baptism, retreated into the wilderness to confront his tempter, while he forged his style of ministry. Finally there was the Transfiguration. Tradition places this on Mount Tabor, rising 1800 feet above sea level, not sheer and dry and rocky like Sinai, but much more moist, mist-shrouded, verdant, but still mysteriously holy.

There is simply something about the mountains that opens up the sensitive soul in the silence. There's something about the wilderness that is different, it is hostile, scary, demanding, that demands careful attentiveness. But here's the amazing thing, it's unexplainable. When we are there, and give ourselves to the silences, abandon any selfish claims on God, and move beyond all our notions of God, let go our childish notions of an old man on a throne with a white beard, without any answers, in deep humility, we know we are loved, and life is good.

It is as if the landscape itself teaches us that as we abandon a frantic search for God, God is there all the time, powerful, awesome, mysterious, just, and loving. As Charles Wesley put it in one of his great hymns, "Thy nature and thy name is Love."

Out there in the wilderness, or in the wilderness of your own heart, when we soak up the Scriptures and turn to the silences, when we come hungry and thirsty for worship and ready for service, when we remember the Jesus revealed on the mountain, we can know the holy God who was behind Jesus and in Jesus. Once you've had the experience God will forever lure you and drive you to a greater vision of peace and holiness and abundance, to a deeper consciousness of humankind and to a compelling love that may yet transform a weary, bloody world.

When I was 63 and my knees were worn out, I was having my last backpacking experience over that same trail, descending a trail near the Continental Divide, when I fell three times. There was no serious injury, but I knew I was facing a crossroads. (It doesn't take a whole lot to get our attention!) I knew I had to do some thinking and decide where I was with respect to this whole enterprise. I knew that my time of backpacking and climbing was coming to an end.

The next day after lunch I stayed back and let the rest of the group go ahead. Johnson Creek was about nine miles away on an easy downhill slope. Beautiful cliffs were rising on both sides, and a lovely stream meandered down the valley. I knew that 41 years of my life of backpacking in the high Colorado Rockies, one of the richest portions of my life was ending. My mood was heavy with grief. So I walked along and stumbled, felt the pack was too heavy and the road was too long. I wept a little while for the vital part of my life that was dying. I talked to the cliffs and they gave me back their silent, indifferent comfort. *Fierce landscapes teach God's love.* Suddenly, as I was walking along, unbidden, the God who speaks in the silence of our thoughts came to me and spoke to me, "My son, it is all right, there are other ways you can see my mountains. You can keep to the old mining roads, you can camp out at the trail heads, you can come by horseback, and when you are very old, you can sit on the porch and be renewed by your very gaze. Don't fret, my son, I am with you."

And God *was* with me, and by his grace I have lived another 20 years and have done all those things. But that day as I walked along and the conversation occurred, the tears dried up, the step seemed steadier, the pack was a little lighter, and in my head I was planning how I would tell the kids that night at campfire that I'd be leaving the next morning. Once again, holy mystery materialized, a harsh and unforgiving environment spoke to an ordinary man about the ordinary balance of life and the ordinary aging process, spoken in the silent voice of a loving God, and the future opened.

"And a voice came from the cloud, 'This is my son, the beloved, listen to him.'" And the same voice says the same to us across these centuries, "listen to him," and if you do, the voice you hear may well be the voice of the God of the mountains.

One of Chappell's poems, written in 1990, is called "We Go to the Mountains:"

> We go to the mountains
> for so much more
> than just vacation,
> mere diversion, seeing sights.
> Oh yes.
> We go, to know
> first hand earth's beauty
> and the Beauty of the One
> who made it,
> in Whose mountains
> souls are lifted with their gaze.
>
> We go, to sleep
> against the bosom
> of an alpine meadow,
> to lie beneath
> the brilliant, countless
> near-by stars,
> snug in our sleeping bags

against night's chill,

to talk ourselves to slumber
on mother earth's soft shoulder.
We go, to sense
our own createdness,
along with all we see and touch;
also our finitude,
we who will to dust return.
We go, to know the God
who from the dust
brought us to breath.
(Oh Mystery! Oh Wonder!)

We go, to taste
the sweetness
of a cold, clear mountain brook,
to stand in awe before a waterfall,
remembering our origin
within the sea
and that we still
are 98 percent sea water.
We go, to breathe
a purity the city
doesn't know,
above, beyond pollution's haze.
We go, to be restored
in living troth
with conservation,
vowing we shall leave
this earth more pure,
committed to her preservation
and protection.

We go, to find our humbling,
our corrected context,
putting self into
perspective 'gainst

the ageless ranges.
We go, to find ourselves,
to leave behind
our insulation from encounter—
the stuff, the things
the walls and concrete,
the packages and pressures—
out there, unencumbered,
reduced to elementals
food tents our feet and legs,
each other
and some time together.

And finding deeper self
we find as well the God
who leads us back below
to service lives,
more whole and human,
Spirit touched,
renewed,
transformed.
That's why we go.

Appendix: Poetry

LEISURE

I see a frantic dashing
all around the clock
in search of meaning.
So many people work
as though possessed of demons,
and then go forth to play
the same, bewitched.

Others find a boring dullness
in their work,
and may revert to
time away from work
to find their meaning.

Some find neither work nor play
to be appealing,
and spend their years
pathetically in apathetic flatness.

Anything you do
which makes you new
and whole is leisure.

It's not a case of simply
time away from work,
but rather quality of using
all the time of life,
knowing one is summoned
to the living by the Giver,
and called to stand accountable
for how one stewarded
His gift.

Full fortunate are those who
find a quality of joy
and creativity in *all* they do,
whether on the job or mowing grass,
or buried in a favorite book,
or quietly at conversation
with a friend.
(Camp Reynoldswood, Dixon, Illinois, February 10, 1971)

ON BEING ME

A "fundy" friend (fundamentalist)
jumped on me hard
with both his feet,
that I was too self-confident,
autonomous, and didn't dribble
holy language all the time.
(My way of putting it,
but what he meant.)

My answer now:
(I didn't think it,
flustered, then when
he attacked! I rarely do!)

I have to do it my way;
I have to live within

the Light God gives
  to me.

But this I see
with utter clarity,
it is the God who was in Christ
who lights my light,
who models modes of being,
who checks my swing,
and in whose Love
  I live and move.
Even my autonomy
comes as his Gift,
    and call.
It's He who gives the right
  to do it my way!
    (May 8, 1973)

ON TRAIL

The other day
I once again
committed all my
life and service
yet remaining
to the Lord.
It was a strange
adventure—
breaking camp
at Vallecita Creek (Va-yeh-see-ta)
and hiking under
pack alone toward
Columbine—
others quite a ways ahead
while some remained
to button down
the camp.

For reasons unaccountable
I suddenly came tearful:
the rain that ruined
half the trail of yesterday
and last night's sleep?
the heavy pack?
the trail awinding
up and up and up?
the universal human
inner loneliness?
Or, part of all of these
combined with
such profundity
of boundless gratitude
for God's amazing
wondrous blessing
of my life,
which somehow seemed
to concentrate into
the essence of that
Rocky Mountain moment?

And so I wept,
and gave myself
to him again
for all my days—
to love, to serve,
to spend myself
that others know
the fullness of the life
he's given me.
    (August 16, 1972)

COLORADO IN THE FALL

How do you capture
Colorado in the Fall

(or trap a scenic splendor)
into merely printed words?
No way. That's all.
But grateful poets with the gall
to try, must try:

One first is struck
by variegated hues of frosted aspen,
from summer's brighter green
by fading into paler shades
'till merged with gentle
yellows which reverse the trend
by toning up to brilliant gold,
touched here and there with copper.
Only seeing is believing.

Then put this tinted splatter
salt on pepper,
intertwined with darker spruce
on circling mountain valleys
to the farthest view,
and up above,
the rocky crested heights,
while far beyond
the massive peaks and ranges
flecked and daubed
with early snow
like graying stalwart troopers
marching row on row.

To Jeep the lonely
long-abandoned miner's trails
is thrill enough for frail
or stouter hearts.
We furthermore compounded
all our awe
by flying overhead
in small one engined bird,

and saw below
some cosmic mad Van Gogh's
colossal frenzied piece:
the ancient tortured surface
he had now collaged
with gentling molding mixes
in indescribable and colorful array.
Only seeing is believing.
Back below
the brilliant alpine flower garden
was already past.
A multitude of grasses
stood in place,
inviting dry arrangements
fit to grace
the castle of a prince.

The roaring fireplace thawed
the ice from early dawn,
though brilliant sun
did diamond glistening crystals
in the morning frost,
and nooned the lawn so warm
bikinis blossomed for a tan.
At evening time a lower flame
brought sweatered comfort
for the quiet conversation
of dear friends,
a glass of wine,
a Hi-Fi tape of Strauss,
combine for holiday sublime.

Freed from the rush of work,
the sting of air pollution,
the gloom of daily news,
one's mind reviews
the qualities that really matter.

And one returns to work
and life possessing all,
from Colorado in the Fall.
    (October 10, 1970)

AND THERE ARE FLOWERS

If you must journey
thru the darkest night
   of soul,
if you are called to travel
   lonely,
   frightened,
   empty,
   lost,
then hear the news
from one who's gone
that road before:

day comes after night
dark's dispelled by light
and there are flowers,
   grass,
the trees,
and me.
    (April 27, 1973)

SELF INTEREST

The most abundant source
of human energy
that I have seen
begins to flow
when someone gets
in touch with what
he really wants to do.
Of me it's true.
And, furthermore,

I've seen it happen
time again to persons
and to groups.

I'm learning ways
to let it happen—
a help that's much too wise
to soberly advise
 some seeker—
but help more like a midwife
to the birthing of another's
living, inner power.
(April 17, 1973)

IT TAKES ALL KINDS

I may not like it
but it takes all kinds
of human beings.

Some quirk in me
when—once a younger preacher
led me to dead sure certainty:
things *had* to be the way I saw them,
and those who disagreed were wrong!
If only they could see it my way
how much finer this old world would be!
Surely God was right
to make it all so clear to me.
Why did he not
make his will
as equally distinct to others?
Why could they not see
that what I saw was right?
The shaping circumstance
which molded
my convictions
seemed to me God's plan

for man!

But now I've changed my tune,
in part from living—
long enough
to see—
in painful outline
blunders I have made,
and integers of truth
that I mistook for sums.
It takes all kinds, indeed.
Some one need counterbalance me!
And thee!

For each who lives this life
in search of his most certain truth
can only see the light
thru screened perceptions finite,
filtering his view.
Hence if mankind would see
life whole he needs
must piece together many personal
fragments of perception into a full mosaic.

No one alone possesses
all the chips of truth.

Let's add the sum
to make the picture whole,
for whether we do
like it well or not,
and whether by divine design or chance,
it takes all kinds.
    (April 26, 1973)

I DIDN'T THEN TAKE OFF MY SHOES

A score of years ago while

early in my journal-writing era
I drove to Baltimore
to take another workshop
in the Progoff method.
Conducted in the meeting room
of formerly a Roman Catholic
seminary, 200 crowd into
a classroom full of writing chairs
with foldup right-armed desks.
Near me sat a nun,
homely as an aged pugilist,
blind as an anvil
and as stout,
yet with a beatific smile,
sublime, serene demeanor
not a soul could miss.
She wrote her journal entries
with a one-hand Braille machine
on rolls of calculator tape
as fast as we with eyes and pen.
She even took her turn
at reading out aloud her entries,
fingers speeding over tape
as fast as we with sight!
A truly liberated soul
delivering an utterly
remarkable performance,
triumphant spirit, barely
slowed by blindness while
led by inner sight.

All then that I could register
was just a low-keyed
"Interesting!"
It took me twenty years
to see the wondrous work
unfolding at my elbow.
But now, past seventy and six

I am amazed and struck with awe!
Multilayered unbelievable display!

Thank you, God, for such a sight!
Thank you, God, that *now* I see:
that next such happening occur
I'll know it then,
take off my shoes that instant,
aware I stand on holy ground.
    (December 7, 1996)

THE UNEXPECTED (A Christmas poem)

One dull December day
when I was lower than
the heavy laden sky,
I slowly came aware
that I was tired of Christmas.

The carols in November'd turned
to songs for stimulating sales;
the decorations—
secular, irrelevant and trite;
commercialized by profit quest,
the One by prophet bards foretold
was hidden in a plastic mess;
and I was worn from
empathizing with
the weariness of clerks.

    Right then
the miracle of Birth
    occurred
the billionth time.
Surprise! Great gift!
A line from some
subconscious carol
amplified to shoppers

stabbed my being
wide awake to Incarnation:
the well-worn words,
it suddenly occurred,
spoke none the less of Him!
In me He came again
    right then!
O wondrous day
Of God's redeeming lift!

Perhaps that's how
he always comes:
the long-expected Jesus
Christ arrives disguised
in what is unexpected—
where he was
not supposed to come—
at unanticipated time—
to pierce our dullness
    full away,
to bring out into
the sunshine of God's love,
to feel again the warmth
and everlasting joy
    of Christmas.
        (December, 1972)

ON HAPPENEDNESS OR TRUTH

Of the stories, legends, lore
his people told, an old Seattle chief
once smiled a knowing smile and said,
"They may not all have happened,
but they're true!"
And now some scholars raise historic questions
of the fact and fiction
    in the Gospels:
    Were there really angel choirs?

A star, parade of shepherds,
visit from the seers?
Old Simeon and Anna
identifying baby Jesus at his
temple presentation as The One
who would redeem a captive Israel?
Dear Friend of Faith,
if you are stuck
at such a hermeneutic barricade,
look for the Truth of Life,
and not at death by skepticism:
Has the great redeeming power
of God flowed in your soul?
Has Jesus come to dwell
transformingly within your heart?
Oh, yes, you say! Then you can
move beyond bare happenedness
to vibrant living truth.
And cherish Christmas love.
    (Christmas 2002)

DISPARITY: A PRAYER

O God, please help me understand
the great disparity 'tween what
I see needs doing in the world
and my own limitations.
The suffering around the world
quite numbs imagination
and paralyzes our compassion;
at times I cannot stand
the terrifying incompletion
of so many lives
(my own included).
Up against all this there comes
my clear repeated call
(so inescapable)
to make a difference,

and then I weep in laying out
my tiny clout
beside the massive need.
I ache to lift the burdens,
I long to fill the voices,
to teach the ignorant,
to heal the suffering,
stop destruction,
build community,
preserve the ecosystem,
and foster wide fulfillment.

Why do I see it all so vast,
and yearn to get it changed
yet wield such puny power,
struggle with an ordinary intellect,
and live reminded of my failures?

Oh, help me, God!

Lord, are you teaching me
my lessons in humility?
Are you leading me to roles
that are appropriate for me?
Is my work in the talk
(spurred by the pain
of such a raw disparity),
to paint the picture
with my words
(words I have belittled?)

I'm at an age when
strength for action wanes,
and leisure in my latter years
allures and beckons.
(Oh, help me, God.)

Is then my call

to see it big,
to hold the hurt within
as goad to tell it out
in summons, that others,
younger, stronger, more in power,
will enter into service?

Speak to me, Lord,
in my disparity.
    (October 24, 1992)

BECAUSE MY NAME IS LOVE

I'm thinking of my life,
of where I am
at this specific stage:
my work, my age,
our family's stable growth,
our home, my books,
my reading, study, deep reflection,
the inner journey, spirit quest,
a sometime flow of poetry
to my amazement,
the workshops, teaching
        preaching
just enough for keeping
energy aflowing,
an income adequate
to save a bit for latter years,
remarkable good health,
a coterie of friends
who bless me
far beyond deserving,
a radiantly beautiful companion
whose very presence
graces every day,
a certain confidence
my trust in God

is soundly founded,
and faith that
Providence secures
the eons yet to come.

I'm humbled,
    awed,
bewildered, asking
"Why me, Lord?"
What have I done
For blessings oh so bounteous?"
And back across
deep consciousness
the answer comes,
"It's not what you
have done, My Son;
I love you just because
my name is Love."
    (March 24, 1990)

GROWING OLDER

I can't adjust
to the face I see
that's always looking
back at me
from each chance glance
or plated window
as I pass.
I just don't know
this aged guy
with snow on top,
with baggy eye
and saggy crop.
Though he's been sneaking
into view for several years,
the visage always startles,
and repels.

I don't like him.
Never will.
I'll make no peace
with getting old.
They'll drag me,
kicking, screaming,
to my wheeling chair.

You see, the me
in dreams at night
      is teen
or young adult!
Never this old guy
the mirror shows,
who suddenly appearing shakes
me up, producing
double takes
and sober thoughts.
I much prefer
the me of memory,
whose hair is dark,
whose knees both work,
whose face is tight,
who hasn't bulges
here and there.
Growing old
just came too fast.
A score of years
all disappeared
in some black hole
that swallows up our days.

Oh I can see
what really is:
I'm now beyond
the proverb's
three-score-ten,
I've danced the dance
and now my body's

paying off the piper:
I loved the rounds,
the turning allemandes,
the times and figures,
the beats and changes.
Oh, yes, I gave
the dancing-that-was-life
a mighty turn.
With no regrets.
In retrospect
it was a glorious cotillion.

I thank the gracious Lord
Who gave not just the life
but also drive and strength
to live it to the hilt.
So why resent
this older stranger who appears?

I guess I deeply wanted life
to last forever.
I've loved the living
much too much.
It's my idolatry.

So let me now,
Dear God, give that same
whirl to loving You,
Who gave me life,
the tunes, the rhythm and
a yearning for the dance,
and also gave the limitations.
Not that I'd love life the less,
nor giving less of self,
but loving You the most.
And 'chance by special grace,
another gift, to learn

to love the me
I see in mirrors.
    (December 13, 1990)

FRANK WILSON CHAPPELL, JR.: 1916-1998

My older brother died today.
My thoughts are deeply stirred.
I was churchier than he,
More mystic, more readily believing;
And he more literary, skeptical,
A journalist, more worldly.
He'd seen things covering cops
As cub reporter that I would never see,
And he was much more into drama,
novels, biography, and theater;
well-informed on history,
student of the Civil War,
he'd tramped the battlefields;
one very widely read,
well-grounded conversationalist.

But growing up as kids
(he older three years and a half)
is how I vividly
remember him as
very worthy older brother,
teacher, guide, protector.
He read to me
From Robin Hood,
From Earnest Thompson Seaton's
Little North Woods Savages,
From "Field and Stream"
and "Outdoor Life."
We dreamed great boyhood dreams
Of wilderness adventures
which waited 40 years to

come reality for me.
When told at 6 that adults
"did it," and that's where
babies came from, I cried,
and hit the kid and screamed,
"My mother and daddy
wouldn't do that," he gently brought the truth,
with understanding, so
I survived the moral bruise.
When adolescence came,
And genitalia grew in size,
He it was explained
"men keep them on the left side,"
and other elemental human wisdom
not in the school curriculum.
He always seemed to know
the right way we should go,
a very worthy older brother,
teacher, guide, protector.

We played the woods, the fields,
the creeks out on the edge
of Dallas, way back before
the city's northward surge.
We saw a bulldog
fight a water moccasin.
We captured pigeons
in an old abandoned barn
by flashlight in the night,
and had a massive roast.
His brandnew Christmas handax just
demanded cutting something:
we chose a creekbed tree immediately
behind the township city hall!
Policemen hauled us into court,
scared spitless, 7 and 10,
to promise we would never

ever sin again.
When I was 16 playing center
on the football team,
and he was home from college
for a game that ended in a melee,
before I knew the fight was on
I took my stance to snap the ball
the last play of the game,
he quickly vaulted from the stands
and stood there at my side,
middle of the 40 yard line,
hustling several of us out of danger.

I say, a very worthy older brother,
teacher, guide, protector.

College and career took us afar,
though I believe we shared
a pride for what the other did.
I know I loved to list
his honors, recognitions
and accomplishments, not the least
of which was being such a marvelous
older brother, husband, son and father,
as well as master journalist.

I've fussed at God
for letting his last years
deteriorate in agony
and useless loneliness.
It wasn't fair.
I can't explain.
I'm only thankful now
his torture's over.
I trust him to a gracious God
for whom he searched but never found,
in whom he wanted vainly to believe;
yet one who knows the righteous gentle core

of his so useful being.
Farewell, good brother, fare you well.
I'll miss you just as deeply
as the world will miss your worth;
a very worthy older brother,
teacher, guide, protector.

MEMORIAL SERVICE

Memorial service for a friend;
remembering her gifts,
her humor constant to the end,
a radiant accomplished life.

Am I hurting for her death?
or for her husband
now alone, also a friend?
Or do I grieve in selfishness
for my own loss?
Since any death reminds

again of *my* mortality,
as hers recalls the emptiness
her passing brings to *me*,
I wonder why I grieve?

For those who die?
their unfulfilled potential?
the loss to humankind?
Or is it that thereby
our own mortality
our own impending end
is clearly intimated?
Or does our grieving
show a lack of faith,
a void within our trust
that brings us fearful
and uncertain, contemplating

what's ahead?

Oh that our grieving
serve a worthy purpose,
a deeper healing,
and call us to renewal,
to higher authenticity,
that we shall truly
rest in God,
beyond all questioning
and fear.
(February 5, 1991, at the service for Madele Terry Hares)

ONE CANNOT WILL ONESELF ANOTHER SHAKESPEARE (condensed)

I yearn to be transparent,
perchance to touch another
with a sunrise
that enables fuller living,
or closer walk with God.
That I am neither
numbered with the greats
of mind and spirit
nor those of giant literary skill
is simply as it is!
The only thing I have a corner on

is being me. I'm good at that.
It would be wonderful
if I were great,
but I am only me,
and I can live with that.

One is given greatness.

Greatness isn't chosen.
I cannot say things
more significant

than what I am in fact.

If plain sincerity
touched by transparency
proscribes my outer limits,
so let it be.
One cannot will oneself
another Shakespeare.
But I can will to walk
with Holy Love, with Holy Mystery,
with Mystic Presence, Truth, and Justice,
then tell my tale
as it is given *me* to tell.
        (January 16, 1999)

Afterword

Recounting the life of a person such as Wally Chappell can have several lessons. It can be an inspiration for others to utilize their talents as fully as is possible and to seek to lead a life that is fulfilling in its own right as well as helpful to others. Such as life will not only have a spiritual base but will include study, travel, physical exercise, and strong involvement in the community and world about us.

Chappell's story can move us beyond the narrow, parochial identification many of us have with our community, our nation, and our version of religion, to take a more cosmopolitan and universalistic attitude towards other nations, religions, other racial and ethnic groups. In a world that is becoming smaller, such a view may be imperative.

His story is also a reminder that our lives are intricately intertwined with others. To review how Chappell was influenced by his parents, his siblings, his teachers, his wife and others underscores how all of us are influenced by many people. It would take a long time to trace the influence of this man on those with whom he has made contact. The story of Al Slaton in chapter one is only one example. Not only did Chappell influence this man, but he in turn has been able to help many others.

In terms of theology, this story is a reminder that an authoritarian, rigid faith is inadequate to reach people in the 21st century. Christians will not all agree on the proper emphases of their faith, and that is at it should be. But as Christianity (or any religion) seeks to speak to a scientific, skeptical world, a faith that is open to insights from all sources is most likely to have an appeal.

Finally, there is a message here about the church. That many moderns find the church boring and irrelevant is beyond dispute. A church that is essentially a local club that is most concerned about its own interests will not survive very long. The church is called to be a living, active embodiment of fellow seekers who do not claim to have all the truth, but who reach out in openness to others, and who seek to implement the implications of their faith to the community and world about them.

Related Reading

Chappell, Wallace E. "I'm Peddling as Fast as I Can." *Circuit Rider*, June 1987: 3-5.

Copeland, Warren E. *And the Poor Get Welfare: The Ethics of Poverty in the United States.* (Nashville: Abingdon Press, 1994.) Good study of poverty in this country. Chapter 9 is a cogent discussion of process theology.

Girard, Rene. *Violence and the Sacred.* Baltimore: John Hopkins University Press, 1990.

Hares, James. *Blest Be Our Ties: A History of the North Texas Conference.* (United Methodist Church, North Texas Historical Project, 2000.) Valuable history of the conference with several references to Chappell around page 100.

Howell, Leon. *United Methodism @ Risk: A Wake-Up Call.* Kingston, New York, 2003: Information Project for United Methodists. Much of chapter 4 of Howell's work is used in Chappell's discussion of the church (chapter 8).

Miller, Robert Moats. *Harry Emerson Fosdick: Preacher, Pastor, Prophet.* New York, Oxford: Oxford University Press, 1985.) Biography of another progressive minister, perhaps the best-known in the twentieth century.

Outler, Albert. *The Wesleyan Theological Heritage: Essays of Albert Outler*. Grand Rapids, Michigan: Zondervan, 1991. The late theologian on his idea of the quadrilateral and other matters.

Phillips, Kevin. *Wealth and Democracy: A Political History of the American Rich*. New York, Broadway Books, 2002.

Pieper, Josef. *Leisure: Basis of Culture*. New York: Pantheon Books, 1963.

Progoff, Ira. *At a Journal Workshop the basic text and guide for using the intensive journal*. New York: Dialogue House Library, 1975.

Tillich, Paul. *The Shaking of the Foundations*. New York: Charles Scribner's Sons, 1948. This collection of Tillich's sermons is a good introduction to his thought. See especially the sermon entitled "You Are Accepted."

Wink, Walter. *Engaging the Powers: Discernment and Resistance in a World of Domination*. Minneapolis: Fortress Press, 1992.

Glossary of Terms

Annual Conference: a structure within Methodism that encompasses an entire state or a segment of a state. All ordained ministers in that geographic area are members of the Annual Conference, and local churches elect representatives to be members so that the conference has approximately 50 percent ministers and 50 percent laymen.

appointment: an assignment by a bishop of a person to be the pastor of a church or to hold another position, such as chaplain. The cabinet is involved in making appointments on an annual basis.

apportionments: suggested amounts of money that each Methodist church is asked to raise during a conference year to support the larger ministry of the church and to go to missions and other outreach causes. (Local outreach programs are separate from apportionments.)

bishop: the highest official of the Methodist Church. A bishop is a minister who is elected at a Jurisdictional Conference. Normally there will be one or two bishops for each state.

board: see general board.

Book of Discipline: the book of law of the United Methodist Church. It is the instrument for setting forth the laws, plan, polity, and process by which United Methodists govern themselves.

cabinet: the bishop of a particular area and the district superintendents, acting together.

canon: the generally accepted listing of books that are considered scriptural.

charge conference: the annual business meeting of a local church.

connectional system: the arrangement in some churches, including Methodism, in which all churches are related to all others, and the church is governed by rules and principles that apply to the whole denomination.

creed: a formulation of faith. The best known is the Apostles' Creed (though not written by the apostles), but there have been many, including some from the contemporary era.

district superintendent: a minister assigned to preside over a district, a geographic portion of an Annual Conference. A district superintendent is the pastor of the ministers in his or her district, and has an advisory role in making appointments.

ecumenical: an inclusive philosophy of cooperation with other denominations, stressing that the things the groups agree on are more important than what they disagree on. An ecumenical attitude also favors contact with the major world religions.

fundamentalism: an ultra-conservative theological position which holds that the words in the Bible are inerrant. It strongly affirms what it considers to be historic doctrines of the church. Fundamentalism as an organized movement dates from the early 20th century.

general board: a structure of a denomination, such as Methodism, that carries out study and activities within a specific area, such as education or missions, for the entire denomination.

General Conference: the highest legislative body in the Methodist Church, which meets in the spring once every four years. It is composed of an equal number of lay and clergy delegates elected by their annual conferences. Only the General Conference can speak for the entire Church.

heresy: a significant deviation from orthodoxy.

hierarchy: a bureaucratic (vertical) structure in a body such as the Roman Catholic Church or the United Methodist Church.

Jurisdictional Conference: a conference set in a regional part of the country, such as the Southeast or Far West, which meets once every four years. One of its main duties is to elect bishops.

lectionary: a prepared document that suggests Biblical and preaching topics for each Sunday in the Church year. It is prepared by an ecumenical committee of 20 denominations, including the Roman Catholic Church.

locate: retire (applied to ministers, especially in the past)

Methodist Church: see United Methodist Church.

Nashville: a symbol of the hierarchal structure of Methodism, because the United Methodist Publishing House and some general boards are located in Nashville, Tennessee.

National Council of Churches: principal ecumenical agency of Christians in the United States. Founded in 1950. It includes 36 denominations from Protestant, Anglican and Orthodox churches, including the United Methodist Church.

ordination: the conferring of ministerial status by a bishop on a minister, with the laying on of hands and the use of a certain liturgy. A person can be licensed to preach without having full ordination. Women have been eligible for full ordination in the United Methodist Church since 1964.

orthodoxy: generally accepted beliefs of a religion or denomination.

pacifism: a philosophy of nonviolence. Pure pacifists eschew war or violence altogether, while others grant a defensive use of force in limited cases.

parsonage: a home or apartment provided by a local church for the use of its minister and family, as long as that minister is under appointment to that church. In recent years, some churches provide a minister a fund with which to buy a home.

Pastor-Parish committee: the committee in the local church that concerns itself with the status of the minister(s) at that church. They make recommendations concerning the minister's staying or moving.

pietism: a religious faith that stresses emotion and warmth.

quadrilateral: a view of authority attributed to the late theologian Albert Outler that considers scripture, tradition, reason, and experience as the bases for our faith.

progressive: a movement to make churches more flexible in doctrine and more relevant to the society. Opposed to fundamentalism.

United Methodist Church: the denomination established by John Wesley in England, breaking from the Anglican Church. It took root in the United States in 1784 and became the second-largest Protestant denomination in the country. At one time it broke into the Methodist Episcopal Church, North, the Methodist Episcopal Church, South, and the Methodist Protestant Church. The three groups united into the Methodist Church in 1939. Then the group united with the Evangelical United Brethren Church in 1968 and took its present name.

universalism: a theological position that believes that all persons will eventually be claimed by God. It opposes a rigid division between heaven and hell.

About the Author

C Emory Burton is a sociologist (Ph.D., The University of Tennessee, Knoxville) and a retired minister of The United Methodist Church, having served churches in Alabama and Indiana. As a minister, he worked to relate religious faith to the community and larger world. Burton's specialty in Sociology is poverty and hunger, and he has written a textbook in this field, two book chapters, and several articles in the religious and secular press. He and his wife Dorothy live in Dallas, Texas, and attend the First United Methodist Church, where they came to know Wally Chappell.

Printed in the United States
125392LV00003B/370-417/A